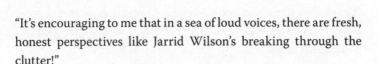

WORDS OF PR...
JESUS SWA...

"It's encouraging to me that in a sea of loud voices, there are fresh, honest perspectives like Jarrid Wilson's breaking through the clutter!"

— Jon Acuff, *New York Times*
best-selling author of *Do Over*,
Start, and *Stuff Christians Like*

"What Jarrid does have here is a book that lays it out there for all of us to realize that living a life for Jesus isn't something we're to be ashamed of. It's something to be proud of. To live for. To die for. I love this book!"

— Judah Smith, *New York
Times* best-selling author
of *Jesus Is _____*.

"Jarrid Wilson is a fresh and powerful new voice in the church today. His call to authentic faith is something we should all listen to and learn from. I'm grateful for how he models the walk of faith."

— Jud Wilhite, author of
Pursued, senior pastor of
Central Christian Church

"*Jesus Swagger* is a punch to the gut of mediocre Christianity."

— Matt Wade, pastor at
Cross Point Church

"Readers beware: Jarrid Wilson doesn't pull any punches. If you are a poser preacher, bogus believer, or faker follower who wants to be left alone to live an inauthentic life pretending to be someone you're not, stay as far away from this book as possible. *Jesus Swagger* will kick you out of your comfort zone, force you to face your fears, and catapult you into a more honest existence. Put it down right now so you can keep being the impostor God never called you to be."

— Jonathan Merritt,
author of *Jesus Is Better
than You Imagined*

"I'm excited about this book! My friend Jarrid has written a super book. *Jesus Swagger* is a call to love and action. You'll be glad you bought this book."

— Derwin L. Gray, lead pastor
of Transformation Church,
author of *Limitless Life: You
Are More Than Your Past
When God Holds Your Future*

"Finally—a book that acknowledges the distinction between a religious poser and someone who actually looks like Jesus. I've been waiting a long time for a book like this, and I bet you have too."

— Jeff Goins, author of
The Art of Work

"For many of us, there is a gap between the relationship with God we have and the relationship with God we thought we'd have when we first started following Jesus. The Christian life we're living isn't what we'd thought it would be. We lost our swagger. *Jesus Swagger* closes that gap and reintroduces us to a Jesus that loves us with a transformative love. Read this book. Fall in love with Jesus all over again. Be a part of His life-changing movement."

— Justin Davis, author of
*Beyond Ordinary: When a
Good Marriage Just Isn't
Good Enough*, pastor at
Cross Point Church

"Too often, Christians get caught up speaking their own language, and have trouble communicating the gospel in the language of culture. In the wake of Jesus and the apostle Paul, Jarrid redeems culture's lingo to teach a new generation how to love Jesus well. As he does with hundreds of thousands of followers on social media, Jarrid boldly, clearly, and wittingly points to the amazing gospel in this book, and helps you see where you may or may not be faking your faith, so you can learn to love Jesus for real. The world can get things so wrong. We ourselves, without the light of Christ, can get things so wrong. Jarrid calls us to true swagger, the greatest way any man or woman can carry themselves: not just talking the talk, but walking the walk. No posers allowed."

— Matt Brown, evangelist, author
of *Awakening* (2015), and
founder of Think Eternity

"Knowing and talking with Jarrid Wilson has not only been a blessing in my life, but I can see and know that what he is doing is going to be a blessing to others. What he is ministering about in *Jesus Swagger* is what people need to hear. It's about being Christ-like and not conforming to the ways of the world. He models his walk with God the same way, letting his Light shine bright."

— Chad Lail, aka Gunner
from Impact wrestling

"Jarrid Wilson helps readers move from being a sideline fan to becoming a passionate follower of Jesus. Wherever you are on your faith journey, *Jesus Swagger* offers a fresh and innovative reality check on whether you're affecting the culture or the culture is infecting you. You're going to hear much from Jarrid Wilson in years to come, get in on the action early and check out this book."

— Margaret Feinberg, author
of *Wonderstruck* and
Fight Back with Joy

"Jarrid Wilson, with authenticity and a heart to lift high the name of Jesus, has written a book that will inspire you to follow King Jesus more completely! As a professional soccer player for the last eight years, it has been a constant struggle to not place my identity in the game. We are not what we do. Instead, we are who God created us to be . . . children of the One true God. Jarrid Wilson communicates this powerful truth in such a refreshing and authentic way. I challenge you to break free from poser Christianity and rock your Jesus Swagger like only you can! This book is a must read!"

— Wells Thompson, Jesus
follower, professional
athlete, and founder of Wells
Thompson Soccer, LLC

JESUS SWAGGER

JESUS SWAGGER

Break Free from Poser Christianity

JARRID WILSON

NELSON
BOOKS

An Imprint of Thomas Nelson

Published in Nashville, Tennessee, by Nelson Books, an imprint of Thomas Nelson. Nelson Books and Thomas Nelson are registered trademarks of HarperCollins Christian Publishing, Inc.

Published in association with Wolgemuth & Associates, Inc.

Thomas Nelson, Inc., titles may be purchased in bulk for educational, business, fund-raising, or sales promotional use. For information, please e-mail SpecialMarkets@ThomasNelson.com.

Unless otherwise noted Scripture quotations are from the *Holy Bible*, New Living Translation, copyright © 1996. Used by permission of Tyndale House Publishers, Inc., Wheaton, Illinois 60189. All rights reserved.

Scripture quotations marked NIV are taken from the *Holy Bible*, New International Version®, NIV®. Copyright © 1973, 1978, 1984, 2011 by Biblica, Inc.™ Used by permission of Zondervan. All rights reserved worldwide. www.zondervan.com

Scripture quotations noted *The Message* are from *The Message: The New Testament in Contemporary English*, by Eugene H. Peterson. Copyright © 1993, 1994, 1995, 1996, 2000. Used by permission of NavPress Publishing Group. All rights reserved.

Scriptures marked ESV are from The Holy Bible, ENGLISH STANDARD VERSION. Copyright © 2001 by Crossway Bibles, a division of Good News Publishers.

Scripture quotations noted NASB are taken from THE NEW AMERICAN STANDARD BIBLE®, Copyright © The Lockman Foundation 1960, 1962, 1963, 1968, 1971, 1972, 1973, 1975, 1977. Used by permission. (www.Lockman.org)

Library of Congress Control Number: 2014951863

ISBN 978-0-7180-2199-3

Printed in the United States of America

15 16 17 18 19 RRD 6 5 4 3 2 1

*To my beautiful wife, loving parents, and
all who have supported my passion to share
the relentless grace of our Lord, Jesus.*

In loving memory of Thomas J. Wilson "Papa"

1943–2013

CONTENTS

INTRODUCTION

WHAT IS JESUS SWAGGER?

~~~

An unconventional man once said, "I got the kind of swagger that you ain't used to."[1]

That man was actually Snoop Dogg (aka Snoop Lion), and catatonic nonetheless, I think he makes a valid point. Although that song goes on to describe subjects I won't mention in this book, that tiny phrase is packed with biblical depth.

It seems that even Snoop Dogg unintentionally understands the basis of Scripture better than most who claim to live their lives by it. As Christians we are called to live like Christ, seek his face, and be a reflection of his love. But for some reason, I truly think we've cracked the very foundation we were called to build upon.

It's one thing to claim a love for God's Word, his commandments, and his divine guidance. But it's a completely different story when one actually tries to live out one's life based on these things. It's the difference between night and day.

In a world of constant conformity, God has called us to be different (Romans 12:2), set apart (Jeremiah 1:5), walking tall with a righteous swagger, a Jesus swagger.

The title of this book explains itself, but does it resonate with you the way it does for me? We talk about being Christlike images, walking as he walked, and talking as he talked, but are we really mirroring that image? Or are we doing the opposite?

To relieve any frustrations you may have from seeing the word *swagger* added to the divine and holy name of Jesus, please understand that the word *swagger* has many meanings, and in this book I plan on referencing the following definition:

"A person's style—the way they walk, talk, dress."[2]

If we evaluate our lives according to the blueprint of Scripture, I believe many of us would be astonished by how much we really *aren't* reflecting the revolutionary example of our Lord and Savior.

Jesus swagger is all about your life being infected with the love of Christ. Being different, *noticeably different*, so much so that people wonder, *What is different about that person?* It's a lifestyle that resembles Jesus to the fullest, not worrying about the opinions of others, but instead holding firm to a foundation in Christ alone; one that is able to withstand anything the world throws at you.

〰

A week before my grandfather passed away, he and I sat in my parents' kitchen while I explained to him what my next book was going to be about. I could see the excitement in his eyes as I began to tell him about what God was stirring in my heart. My grandfather had always been supportive of my ministerial efforts, so much that he even purchased a Kindle just so he and my grandmother could download a digital copy of my first book on release day, before the hard copy was available.

Knowing that my grandfather was truly interested in the concept of my next book, I began to share with him the ideology behind *Jesus Swagger* and why I felt our culture needed to hear this message. My grandfather's face lit up as he listened to me talk, and I'll never forget the confused expression on his face as he asked me, "Wait, what does *swagger* mean again?"

As I proceeded to explain the definition of swagger to my sixty-five-year-old grandfather, I'll never forget the moment he looked at me, chuckled, and stated, "Yup, I've got some of that!" Little did I know that this conversation would be the last that my grandfather and I would ever have.

Two weeks after my grandfather and I sat at my parents' dining table and discussed my upcoming book, he was unexpectedly hit by a car while crossing the street en route to attend a local high school football game—one of his favorite activities. It's crazy to think that it was only a few months back that he and I sat down to discuss what we both believed it truly meant to live like Jesus. And although the mourning of his death was painful and confusing, I can't help but realize that my grandfather was the epitome of someone who harnessed the wondrous likeness of Jesus swagger. Generosity. Self-sacrifice. Openness. Love. Total dependence on God. These things gave him a confidence that went beyond normal swagger, and bordered on something holy.

Jesus Swagger is not just a book, but a road map that will take you through a spiritual journey and make you rethink the way you're living. At the end of your life, how will people know that you lived for Jesus? What about your everyday attitude will leave them wondering about the greatness of God? Will it be the way you treated people? The confidence you walked with? The way you feared God, loved without limits, shared your faith, or modeled Jesus? By the end of this book, I hope you will have already begun evaluating the way you spend your days on this big sphere of dust they call Earth. Jesus didn't die an extravagant death so that we could live mediocre and comfortable lives. The man who gave his life for us expects nothing less than our best, and I don't believe that's too much to give.

Few of us have had the honor of seeing a life that truly lifts the glory and transcendental beauty of Jesus. And while the world continues to see war, darkness, and the pursuit of self-righteousness, the light you give off—your Jesus swagger—could help many down the narrow path you and I are called to walk.

SWAGGER MATTERS

If you think the way you act is irrelevant to your walk with Jesus, you're dead wrong. Not only are your actions viewed as a direct correlation to your relationship with Christ, but people from the outside will always be looking for a flaw to call you out on. I'm not saying this is fair, but I am saying that it's true. If you frequent the national news channels, you'll notice that most of the publicity Christianity seems to get surrounds a group of people who claim to follow Christ, but are doing something irresponsible and hateful, like picketing soldiers' funerals. What are observers supposed to think? Gandhi is often quoted as saying, "I love your Christ, but I dislike your Christianity."[3] Ouch. That hurts. But hey! He just said what everyone else was thinking. From the outside looking in, all he could see was a group of individuals who were unlike the God they were claiming to reflect. How can we let this go on, when we could be the ones to stop it?

The way you walk, talk, and present yourself to others matters when it comes to your faith. Why? Because if you claim to be a Christian, then people are going to expect you to act like one. Simple. Your swagger truly matters. No matter how long or how briefly you've known Jesus as your Lord, you are held to a higher standard of accountability by those around you.

Although there is freedom and grace in the arms of Christ, we are all still called to live above reproach in all that we do. This means that no matter the circumstance, you are called to reflect an image that portrays the purity and boldness of Christ himself. I know that may seem like a tough act to follow, but that's the beauty of the Holy Spirit. God intrinsically designed us to take the Holy Spirit into our lives and allow him to guide and direct us in a way that reflects true Christianity, and to deter us from embracing things that are not from him.

Romans 6:1–20 is one of my favorite passages in the Bible: it depicts the true image of who we are called to be in Christ. In encouraging others to pursue a lifestyle that flees from sin, Paul writes:

> So what do we do? Keep on sinning so God can keep on forgiving? I should hope not! If we've left the country where sin is sovereign, how can we still live in our old house there? Or didn't you realize we packed up and left there for good? That is what happened in baptism. When we went under the water, we left the old country of sin behind; when we came up out of the water, we entered into the new country of grace—a new life in a new land!
>
> That's what baptism into the life of Jesus means. When we are lowered into the water, it is like the

burial of Jesus; when we are raised up out of the water, it is like the resurrection of Jesus. Each of us is raised into a light-filled world by our Father so that we can see where we're going in our new grace-sovereign country. (vv. 1–5 MSG)

We are new! Can you feel that? You and I are new creations, with new hearts, new minds, and new destinations. It's as if God has rerouted us midflight. We are no longer who we once thought we were, but instead who God has called us to be. The paths we have been taking have been repaved with purpose and worth. What a beautiful thing.

Paul goes on to say,

Could it be any clearer? Our old way of life was nailed to the cross with Christ, a decisive end to that sin-miserable life—no longer at sin's every beck and call! . . . Never again will death have the last word. When Jesus died, he took sin down with him, but alive he brings God down to us. From now on, think of it this way: Sin speaks a dead language that means nothing to you; God speaks your mother tongue, and you hang on every word. You are dead to sin and alive to God. That's what Jesus did.

That means you must not give sin a vote in the way you conduct your lives. Don't give it the time of day. Don't even run little errands that are connected with that old way of life. Throw yourselves wholeheartedly and full-time—remember, you've been raised from the dead!—into God's way of doing things. Sin can't tell you how to live. After all, you're not living under that old tyranny any longer. You're living in the freedom of God. (Romans 6:6–14 MSG)

What was once a swagger that thrived off our selfishness has now turned into a Jesus swagger, fueled by a hunger and thirst to reflect the indescribable beauty of Jesus. This uncontainable thirst cannot be quenched by anything of this world, but only through an everlasting relationship with Christ.

Paul goes on:

Well then, since God's grace has set us free from the law, does that mean we can go on sinning? Of course not! Don't you realize that you become the slave of whatever you choose to obey? You can be a slave to sin, which leads to death, or you can choose to obey God, which leads to righteous living. Thank God! Once you were slaves of sin, but now you wholeheartedly obey this teaching we have given you. Now you are free from your slavery to sin, and you have become slaves to righteous living.

Because of the weakness of your human nature, I am using the illustration of slavery to help you understand all this. Previously, you let yourselves be slaves to impurity and lawlessness, which led ever deeper into sin. Now you must give yourselves to be slaves to righteous living so that you will become holy.

When you were slaves to sin, you were free from the obligation to do right. And what was the result? You are now ashamed of the things you used to do, things that end in eternal doom. (Romans 6:15–21 NLT)

So we finally have freedom from the bondage of sin and shame. Yeah, it's a relief. Our mistakes no longer define who we are, but instead we are to find worth in the name of Jesus. But we are not called to take this gift and run, or to ignore God, but to pursue him and thank him for the liberation he has provided us.

Don't waste another moment away from this new righteousness. Don't give your old ways a moment's time. And don't tease yourself by setting foot in your old stomping grounds. You are new, forgiven, and free. Let God's love set your soul on fire.

〰〰

While many individuals live in search of identity and purpose through the acceptance of others, God is impartially waiting for us with open and fulfilling arms. Jesus offers the free gift of eternal salvation, freedom from the bondage of your mistakes, and power to conquer anything that comes between you and your calling. When you embrace this gift, you are able to engage in a swagger that is unlike anything this world can compare to.

WORLDLY SWAGGER	V.	JESUS SWAGGER
Based on image		Based on internal strength from God
Comes and goes with popularity		Stays eternally grounded
Seeks its worth from others		Knows its inherent worth comes from Christ

When one is truly engaged in a relationship with Christ, it is impossible to walk about life unchanged. The old you will slowly be transformed into a righteous individual who seeks justice, grace, and the pursuit of righteous living.

Your life will be radically different when you are transformed as a follower of Christ. You won't be able to recognize yourself in the mirror, but instead you will see a person who has been renewed into someone yearning after the persona of Christ, to express his grace to people. What does that look like? You're more forgiving. You're slower to anger. Your heart breaks with compassion more easily. In this way, when we see injustice, hurt, pain, and hunger, it is as if we are looking through the eyes of Jesus himself.

Jesus swagger is all about embracing the new life that Christ has given us—a life fueled by the power, love, and grace of Christ.

CHAPTER 1

POSER CHRISTIANITY

God is looking for Christ followers,
not religious posers. #JesusSwagger

~~~
~~~

I remember my first day of high school like it was yester-day. The night before was filled with excitement as I dreamed of what could be. I laid out my new clothes for my first day, while continuously giving myself a pep talk about why the next four years were going to be some of the best life could offer.

I guess you could say I had an untainted view of what high school was going to be like. All I could imagine was something resembling a low-budget Disney movie with a hint of *Glee*. Okay, maybe not exactly those things, but I couldn't help but think there might be a few spontaneous dance routines taking place in the halls, and I might even get to see a couple kids getting thrown in their lockers for not bringing the local bully their lunch money.

Regardless, I was excited for the first day of a new adventure, and I think most people my age would have felt the same.

The first day of high school is probably one of the most important days of your high school career. Why? Because the way you represent yourself on day one is quite possibly the way people are going to label you for the next four years. Was I going to be a jock? A geek? A musician? A Jesus freak? A loner? A teacher's pet? The class clown?

I really had no idea who I was trying to be, but all I can remember is staring at the clothes I had purchased the day prior and thinking to myself, *What was I thinking?* I guess I had chosen to go for the stoner-musician look and had also decided to put my faith in the backseat. My parents loved me, but I'd be lying if I said they were extremely fond of my decisions as a teenager.

The reality was, I was accepting the lie that I needed to be someone other than who God had created me to be. All throughout high school, my identity wasn't built upon Christ, but instead the clothes I wore, the friends I had, and the achievements I was trying to gain.

And although I felt very fashion-forward with my long, blond hair, checkered slip-ons, and a T-shirt promoting my favorite band, I'm surprised no one ever told me how ridiculous I looked. Well, maybe someone did, but I obviously didn't take that person seriously.

The truth is, I hated dressing that way, but all the people I planned to spend my time with looked the part, so I figured I would too. It's funny how quickly a friendship can turn into a fashionship, even in ninth grade. But the feeling of being accepted was incredibly hard to resist.

Why? Because our human nature thrives on being accepted and liked by our peers.

Based on the expectations of the world around me, fitting in was something I felt compelled to do in order to "be somebody." Maybe it was the thousands of shallow and scandalous advertisements I saw each day. Or maybe it was the media imposing its lies onto my feeble and newly pubertized brain. Or maybe it was because my heart wasn't grounded in the Word of God, but instead the shallow words of man. I'm pretty sure it was the last one, but regardless, all of those options played a role in my belief that in order to be accepted I had to follow the crowd.

Based on the culture that surrounded me, an outsider was considered uncool, lame, and mediocre. But little did I know that ignoring my identity in Christ made me as mediocre as they come. I was nothing more than a cookie-cutter crowd-pleaser. I was just another cliché. And according to Romans 12:2, I was exactly opposite of who God called me to be. It says, "Don't copy the behavior and customs of this world, but let God transform you into a new person by changing the way you think. Then you will learn to know God's will for you, which is good and pleasing and perfect."

I was conforming to the world without even realizing it. My swagger resembled nothing of Christ and everything to do with creation.

It didn't take long for me to start posing in other attributes in my life: music, movies, books, and even the types of food I ate. I began posing as someone I wasn't, in order to gain acceptance from people.

The worst thing is that I claimed to be a Christian during my entire high school experience. I mean, I attended church, went to Bible study, and even memorized a few verses, but the reality is I never let the message of Jesus completely transform me, nor did I share my faith with others. I clearly remember the times I ignored my relationship with God in order to be part of the crowd. I was so young, but I knew the truth—and chose to ignore it.

But I soon came to realize there is a big difference between knowing *of* him and knowing him personally. Not only was I posing as someone I wasn't with my so-called friends, but I was also posing as a follower of God at the same time. How twisted is that?

It wasn't until years later that I truly began to seek God for who he is, and not who I wanted him to be, that those insecurities started to subside, and my view of God became more selfless rather than selfish.

It's mind-blowing how much of my experience in high school reflects the lifestyle of many self-proclaimed Christians in today's world.

Think about it. How many people in today's world claim to be Christians who love and follow God, but in reality are nothing more than religious posers? They claim to be one thing, but in reality aren't what they seem. My hand is humbly raised, and I'll be the first to admit that this is a daily struggle for me. Everyone deals with the temptation to give off an image that isn't quite true. There is a term for people like this: that's right, it's called being a poser.

Have you ever been called a poser? Although it seems immature and childish, that word packs a mega-punch in today's vulture culture. Everyone is created differently, but how many of us are pretending to be someone of faith in hopes that outsiders won't be able to see our inner decay?

The first step in finding your inner Jesus swagger is to stop posing as a follower, and start living as one. A true relationship with Christ cannot be mimicked, because only in a true relationship with Christ can we find real transformation.

Some of us always carry a Bible, we serve on the greeting team at our church, and we pray before every meal—even while in public. We have our favorite Bible verses tattooed on our forearms, and our refrigerators are covered in Bible-verse magnets. Not to mention our cars are covered in our John 3:16 and WWJD bumper stickers.

Sound familiar? Lots of us think we're doing God a favor by taking part in all these surface-level activities, when in fact God would be more satisfied with our hearts reflecting him more than our cars and fashion trends. That'll preach.

Don't get me wrong; all of these things are great, and there is nothing wrong with any of them. But when our faith in Jesus ends with the way we decorate our public appearance, we need to stop, evaluate ourselves, and realize that we are heading down a road of false assurance. It's not going to get us anywhere. Jesus swagger is about allowing the message of Jesus to penetrate the core of your heart, releasing an overflow of love, selflessness, and servanthood that goes beyond mere appearances, and makes a positive difference.

Your swagger reflects who you are. When we harness a swagger influenced by the power of Jesus, posing as someone we are not will no longer be an option. But when we don't allow Jesus to fully take control of our lives, posing as a Christian is the only option we will really have.

To be honest, it's easy to live in America as a poser Christian. We buy Christian clothing, stickers, accessories, DVDs, and music. We proudly attend church every once in a while, but we never let the message of Jesus change who we are. It's like throwing plant seeds onto a slab of cement. They aren't going to grow roots. They aren't going to get any nutrients. And they aren't going to grow into what they were created for.

Here is something that might sting a little bit: Just because you believe in Jesus doesn't mean you're going to end up with him.

Before you call me a biblical heretic, hear me out.

James 2:19–20 states, "You say you have faith, for you believe that there is one God. Good for you! Even the demons believe this, and they tremble in terror. How foolish! Can't you see that faith without good deeds is useless?" Even the demons believe! And that belief does nothing for them. We must allow Jesus to become more than just a person we believe in; he needs to be a person we also relentlessly follow and hunger to be more like.

Faith without action is a waste of time. Don't just talk about it; act upon it. I hurt at the thought of how many times I have forgotten this vital truth. This passage isn't saying that "works" will get you into heaven, but that your faith should be complemented by action. Jesus' aim was not for us to strive for good intentions, but to live with righteous ambitions fueled by the forgiveness and atonement he gave us on the cross.

The real issue isn't whether our generation is wearing enough bedazzled cross T-shirts; it's whether we are allowing the message of Jesus to root deeper than our wardrobe, blog posts, music playlists, tweets, and Facebook statuses. We've become a tribe of people who rank our faith in a measurement of likes, re-tweets, and memory verses. We need to up our game.

EIGHT DIFFERENCES BETWEEN A BELIEVER AND A FOLLOWER

1. A believer believes in Jesus. A follower honors his commands.

   You believe that there is one God. Good! Even the demons believe that—and shudder. (James 2:19 NIV)
2. A believer reads the Bible when things get tough.

A follower reads the Bible to engage in a deeper understanding of Jesus himself.

> Look to the LORD and his strength; seek his face always. (Psalm 105:4 NIV)

3. A believer prays when things get tough. A follower gives thanks no matter the circumstance.

> Always giving thanks to God the Father for everything, in the name of our Lord Jesus Christ. (Ephesians 5:20 NIV)

4. A believer twists the Bible to fit his or her lifestyle. A follower works to make his or her lifestyle resemble the teachings of the Bible.

> Some of his comments are hard to understand, and those who are ignorant and unstable have twisted his letters to mean something quite different, just as they do with other parts of Scripture. And this will result in their destruction. (2 Peter 3:16)

5. A believer gives when it's easy. A follower gives out of the abundance of his or her heart.

> They all gave out of their wealth; but she, out of her poverty, put in everything—all she had to live on. (Mark 12:44 NIV)

6. A believer conforms under the pressure or culture. A follower holds fast against temptation.

> Therefore take up the whole armor of God, that you may be able to withstand in the evil day, and having done all, to stand firm. (Ephesians 6:13 ESV)

7. A believer will share his or her faith when it's comfortable. A follower will share his or her faith regardless of the scenario.

> And he said to them, "Go into all the world and proclaim the gospel to the whole creation." (Mark 16:15 ESV)

8. A believer knows about Jesus. A follower knows Jesus as his or her Lord and Savior.

> Because, if you confess with your mouth that Jesus is Lord and believe in your heart that God raised him from the dead, you will be saved. (Romans 10:9 ESV)

Many people act like being a poser Christian is okay. Does that make you as frustrated as it makes me? It's not just about those obviously hateful people who are claiming to represent Christ while waving their "God hates f-gs" picket signs and yelling into their wrath-of-God megaphones. It's normal, nonconfrontational people too.

This may sound judgmental, but it's a trap any of us could fall into. Claiming to love Jesus but not following his commandments is like selling a pair of brass knuckles to Mother Teresa. It just doesn't make sense.

When our gospel-centered tweets and faith-driven Facebook posts are stripped away, and we are left with nothing more than our hearts and a face-to-face conversation with God, who are we then?

Francis Chan said, "The irony is that while God doesn't need us but still wants us, we desperately need God but don't really want Him most of the time."[4] That's the difference between knowing *about* God and really *knowing* God. When we know God, we know how much we need him.

I want to help you bridge the difference between being a follower of Jesus and being nothing more than a sideline fan. I want to help you develop your Jesus swagger, rather than the cheap imitation swagger that most of the world thinks is enough.

We can't expect the Jesus swagger to flow when all we know about him are some thousand-year-old statistics we researched on Google. These days, anyone can know *about* Jesus, but what does it take to know him?

The definition of *knowing* someone in the Greek text of the Bible (the word *ginosko*) is more than just an understanding of someone, but rather an intimate and extremely knowledgeable relationship that goes further in detail than that of a simple acquaintance.[5]

We must view our relationship with Jesus to be more than just a shallow bond, but one that is worth putting in our time and energy—all in order to deepen its value and worth. This relationship must be put to the forefront of our hearts.

Through obedience, prayer, study, service, a pure heart, and all the things we'll talk about in this book, you'll become a person who fully belongs to God, and then the real swagger will begin to follow.

CHECK YOURSELF

Think about it: Are we the same people we claim to be in 140 characters or less?

Let me tell you more about my poser days. I was juggling the world and the Word, praying that I was doing enough "good" to be loved by God, but also hoping I was popular enough to be accepted by the world around me. It was actually hindering my relationship with God, and not at all helping it.

I would claim to be the "Christian guy" because I listened to all the top chart Christian bands. Not to mention I went to youth group once a week, wore my WWJD bracelet, and had some virtuous morals that could support my claim.

But when it came time to take part in activities the Bible would deem sinful, I would justify my sin by stating the biggest excuse known to man: "God knows my heart." And maybe follow that up with a good self-pep-talk about why I was a "good person." I'm positive I am not the only one who's experienced this.

There are plenty of self-proclaimed Christians who can quote more Scripture than you ever will, preach the most powerful message you've ever heard, and perhaps even tithe more than most people you know. But underneath the good deeds and pretty words they are nothing more than posers. It's all a show. It's the heart that matters, and I say this from personal experience.

POWER RANGER POSER

Every year we use Halloween as our day to play pretend. And no matter how young or old, we see people getting into their fairy-tale attire and killer zombie outfits.

Although this holiday is often full of innocent fun, one Halloween opened up my eyes to something painful and sorrowful but true. One year when I was a kid, I wanted to dress as the Red Ranger from the *Mighty Morphin Power Rangers*, but all the store had left was a Blue Ranger costume. And if you remember the original Power Rangers correctly, Billy the Blue Ranger was a total nerd. Anyway, against my personal preference, I ended up buying the Blue Ranger costume because it was all they had left. And frankly, my mom and I were tired of shopping. Regardless, for one night of my life I was going to be a Power Ranger, and I didn't care that I was the Blue Ranger, no matter how nerdy he was.

When Halloween came around, I remember looking in the mirror, fully decked out in my Blue Ranger costume, laser pistol, and sound-activated gloves. If I recall correctly, I looked pretty sweet. I remember feeling like I could take on the world or fight anyone who came in my path. The costume I was wearing looked so good that I began to believe I actually *was* a Power Ranger.

So I did what any extremely awesome seven-year-old kid would do: I began practicing my ninja moves in the mirror just in case someone tried to steal my candy or

hurt my parents as we walked through dangerous sub-
urbs of Southern California. As I continued practicing my
advanced ninja techniques, I remember doing an incredibly
off-form ninja back kick against my bathroom sink. All of
a sudden I heard a *smack*! I realized I was on the ground.
My knee had been scraped up by the edge of the bathroom
door, and my head felt like it had been super-punched by
an elephant. To be completely honest, I don't remember
exactly what went wrong, but I do know that the kick did
not go the way I had seen it in last week's episode.

As I sat on my tiled bathroom floor in tears, the blood
began to trickle down the side of my kneecap. And as I
wiped the blood off with a piece of toilet paper, I realized
something incredibly heartbreaking. It was something
that would destroy the hope of any seven-year-old's heart.
I realized at that very moment I wasn't a Power Ranger.
I didn't even have superpowers. I didn't fight crime, nor
did I have an incredibly good-looking sidekick named
Kimberly. I was just a kid in a costume trying to be something I wasn't in hopes I could impress the people around
me and prove I was actually the person the costume had
made me out to be.

When my knee stopped bleeding and my mind had
wrapped itself around what had just happened, I cleaned
myself up and took a good, long look in the mirror.

I remember standing there for a solid fifteen minutes
with the insecurities flooding through my head. *You're
not a Power Ranger*, they said. *I bet the Red Ranger would*

have been able to do that kick. And just as the tears began to trickle down my face once more, my mom peeked her head into the door and said, "Hey, my little Blue Ranger! Are you ready to get some candy or what?"

Fact: moms have a powerful way of making things all better. And although she knew I wasn't the real Blue Ranger, I remember my mom telling me how great my costume looked, and that it was my job to protect us while we were out collecting my bagful of cavities.

While this story has a cute and happy ending, it scares me to think that so many others who share a similar experience won't have the same conclusion. This story is about more than pretending to be a Power Ranger. This story is about the lives of most Christians in today's world.

We dress the part, act the part, and even try our best to walk and talk the part. But how many of us are just playing dress-up? How many of us are trying to live as something we aren't? And, how many of us have turned a beautiful relationship with Jesus into a 24-7 costume party, only to end our days realizing we are not really the people we are pretending to be?

CHAPTER 2

STOP THE EPIDEMIC

No past, present, or future is broken enough to
be kept from the all-consuming grace of God.
#JesusSwagger

~~~

Even if poser Christianity is an epidemic in the Christian faith, is the gospel still being shared? Yes. And are lives still being transformed? Yes. I don't doubt God's power to use all things for his good.

But imagine if everyone who claimed to love Jesus actually did. Imagine if everyone who called themselves a Christian put more effort into serving their neighbors than catering to their selfish wants. You know, if we served because others needed help, not just to check a good deed off our list. Or looking at the church budget and being more worried about people coming to know Jesus as Lord than wondering when your church is going to purchase some chairs that are more comfortable. Imagine if every person who called themselves a Christian actually followed the ways of Christ, and completely turned away from living life for their own desires.

If this happened, we would see world change. We would see nations experiencing hope, cities transforming from the inside out, and churches around the world making disciples and going to extreme lengths to serve their communities.

But we're nowhere close. Don't get me wrong—there are incredible things happening in the name of Jesus. But so much more can be done. Our motives must change. Our focus must be reunited with the gospel. And our passion must be fueled by what God can do through us, not just what he can do for us.

Conferences, books, albums, and T-shirts are wonderful tributes to the kingdom of God. In fact, I love that our generation is doing everything it can to expand its reach. But the essence of Christianity goes beyond publicity: it's the belief that people loving people in the name of Jesus will truly change the world.

THE PHARISEE FAKES

There are some posers in Scripture who rocked robes and giant hats instead of Power Ranger costumes: the Pharisees. I kind of feel bad for these guys. I mean, whenever they get brought up I immediately think, *Great. What arrogant nonsense are they spouting now?* No joke: most of these guys are the epitome of religious posers.

The Pharisees were known as the religious elite, the top dogs, and the high-and-mighty of faith. And although these nicknames sound incredibly awesome, the men who were behind them weren't all too savvy when it came to actually knowing their heavenly Father. Pharisees were known to be righteous and zealous for keeping the law. But their observance and protection of the law was filled with arrogance and hypocrisy. They were prideful and stingy with grace. Judgment was easy for these guys, but refusing to show grace or give second chances was their demise.

In Matthew 23, you will find Jesus teaching to the crowds and his disciples about the problems of hypocrisy. He claimed that although the words of the Pharisees may have been wise, their actions did not match what they preached. He continued by describing what most poser Christians face in today's generation: "Everything they do is for show" (Matthew 23:5).

Jesus was publicly calling out the Pharisees for being religious show-offs who were looking to gain nothing but personal acknowledgment for their actions. They were using their faith and knowledge of the Scriptures as a catalyst for personal popularity. They loved the idea of being extremely religious, but failed to convert that into passion for God himself.

Not only did the actions of the Pharisees hurt their own opportunity for salvation, but their ways of living gave a false reflection of what it actually meant to be a follower of God. The constant judgment and religious entanglement they repeatedly subjected people to was theologically unjustifiable.

What sorrow awaits you teachers of religious law and you Pharisees. Hypocrites! For you shut the door of the Kingdom of Heaven in people's faces. You won't go in yourselves, and you don't let others enter either. (Matthew 23:13)

The Pharisees spent so much time focusing on their outer appearance that they failed to allow the inner transformation to take place. You know, the one thing that actually mattered. It would be similar to someone who buys an old car from a junkyard, completely restores both interior and exterior, and then doesn't put any money into fixing the car's engine. It may look spectacular, but it's not going anywhere. Likewise, we seem to have convinced ourselves that if the outer image looks grand enough, then no one will bother asking about what's actually under the hood.

When we find ourselves being complimented on the outer appearance long enough, it's easy to forget about fixing what's inside. As you can imagine, this is a hindrance to many people who are trying to find true transformation in Christ himself.

Since the Pharisees found themselves in the spotlight of religious appreciation, it's no surprise that their elegant speech and impressive knowledge of the law kept them comfortable and unwilling to push further in their spiritual journey.

Do you want to know how to live a great gospel-centered

life? Just do the exact opposite of everything the Pharisees did. The Pharisees were more focused on impressing each other with spiritual knowledge than actually following the commandments of God, showing grace, or lending out a selfless hand. We have to make an effort to walk that talk.

THE PHARISEES	TRUE FOLLOWERS OF CHRIST
Prayed in public for recognition.	Pray in public because they are unashamed.
Read God's Word for head knowledge.	Read God's Word to deepen their relationship.
Judged people for the sake of judgment.	Lovingly correct people because they care.

THE STONES WE THROW

One of my favorite encounters of Jesus and the Pharisees is found in chapter 8 of the book of John. It's a righteous shutdown that has reverberated through history, and become part of how we deal with accusations even to this day. This story is very popular among those even outside the evangelical crowd, and its ripple effect has spread the grace and love of Jesus from person to person.

> But Jesus went to the Mount of Olives. At dawn he appeared again in the temple courts, where all the people gathered around him, and he sat down to teach them. The teachers of the law and the Pharisees brought in a woman caught in adultery.

They made her stand before the group and said to Jesus, "Teacher, this woman was caught in the act of adultery." (John 8:1–4 NIV)

The Pharisees go straight to pointing out the flaws in the adulterous woman. They don't give Jesus her name, how old she is, or even a background of where she has come from. There is no benefit of the doubt in their eyes. The pharisaical group barges into the temple courts, only to throw a heap of judgment and religious law in the face of a woman who is obviously broken. They demand, "In the Law Moses commanded us to stone such women. Now what do you say?" (John 8:5 NIV).

Hoping to trap Jesus into teaching a law in opposition to theirs, they ask him a question that Jesus answers in glorious form. Not only does Jesus' answer completely baffle the Pharisees, but it firmly convicts them of their own faults. Jesus calls out the Pharisees by playing their own game. Talk about reverse tactics. This one is genius.

They were using this question as a trap, in order to have a basis for accusing him. But Jesus bent down and started to write on the ground with his finger. When they kept on questioning him, he straightened up and said to them, "Let any one of you who is without sin be the first to throw a stone at her." (John 8:6–7 NIV)

Instead of stating whether or not the woman deserved to be stoned based on the laws of Moses, Jesus instead asks whoever can call themselves blameless in the sight of the Lord to cast the first stone. Not only does this put the Pharisees in a state of confusion, but Jesus knows none of them are idiotic enough to claim such blasphemy in the eyes of the public.

> Again he stooped down and wrote on the ground. At this, those who heard began to go away one at a time, the older ones first, until only Jesus was left, with the woman still standing there. (John 8:8–9 NIV)

There are many ideas of what Jesus might have been writing in the sand while face-to-face with the Pharisees that day. Some scholars believe Jesus could have been writing down the sins of the Pharisees, their mishaps, and the secrets they tried to keep from the public. I don't know if we will ever know the truth, but I think this postulation makes perfect sense due to the Pharisees' reaction to Jesus' question. It's a punch in the gut to ask, "Who here is blameless?" and it's a total knock-out to then write the sins of those who were thinking about claiming it.

After the Pharisees drop their stones and remove themselves from the presence of the adulterous woman, Jesus makes another shocking statement.

Jesus straightened up and asked her, "Woman, where are they? Has no one condemned you?" "No one, sir," she said. "Then neither do I condemn you," Jesus declared. "Go now and leave your life of sin." (John 8:10–11 NIV)

He offers the woman grace, forgiveness, and a second chance at life. "Then neither do I condemn you. Go now and leave your life of sin."

Jesus' encounter with the Pharisees and the woman caught in adultery draws such a relevant image for what we face in today's culture. Our world finds it so easy to point out the flaws and failures in one another, but constantly fails to realize that we too have our own closetful of sins and mishaps.

Jesus swagger is all about dropping your pharisaical lifestyle and embracing the reality that everyone deserves a helping-hand grace. You and I were once handed a second chance when we didn't deserve it. Grace is not something we get to control. It was never ours to begin with. The grace of God was given to us when we had nothing to give back, and it's only correct for us to offer it to those who we think may not deserve it as well.

Matthew Henry's *Concise Commentary of Ephesians 2* illustrates the power and undeserved potency of God's transforming grace in each of our lives:

Sin is the death of the soul. A man dead in trespasses and sins has no desire for spiritual pleasures. When we look upon a corpse, it gives an awful feeling. A never-dying spirit is now fled, and has left nothing but the ruins of a man. But if we viewed things aright, we should be far more affected by the thought of a dead soul, a lost, fallen spirit. A state of sin is a state of conformity to this world. Wicked men are slaves to Satan. Satan is the author of that proud, carnal disposition which there is in ungodly men; he rules in the hearts of men. From Scripture it is clear, that whether men have been most prone to sensual or to spiritual wickedness, all men, being naturally children of disobedience, are also by nature children of wrath.

This text may seem pretty harsh, but understand that this was before the grace of God entered into our lives. We are no longer considered children of wrath, but instead sons and daughters of God. The toughness in this text is also the beauty. It showcases the love and grace Jesus provided us when he died on the cross. It is a gift that we did nothing to deserve. The grace he has given us brings a new line of connection to him, one that didn't exist while we were still dead in our trespasses and sins.

What reason have sinners, then, to seek earnestly for that grace which will make them, of children of wrath, children of God and heirs of glory! God's eternal love or good-will toward his creatures, is the fountain whence all his mercies flow to us; and that love of God is great love, and that mercy is rich mercy. And every converted sinner is a saved sinner; delivered from sin and wrath. The grace that saves is the free, undeserved goodness and favor of God; and he saves, not by the works of the law, but through faith in Christ Jesus. Grace in the soul is a new life in the soul.[6]

This reckless and powerful grace has saved us from being children of wrath, and instead opened up the door to God's eternal love and mercy. We have been delivered from our brokenness, and instead set free by the undeserved grace and favor of God.

SIX THINGS JESUS DIDN'T DIE FOR

1. JESUS DIDN'T DIE SO THAT WE COULD TAKE ADVANTAGE OF HIS GRACE.

Grace is never deserved, and it also is not to be taken advantage of. While God's grace flows in abundance, this does not give us the right to misuse it for the benefit of our selfish desires. This doesn't mean we are expected to be perfect, but instead progressing toward real righteousness, God's way (Titus 2:11–12).

2. JESUS DIDN'T DIE SO THAT WE COULD REFLECT CHRISTIANITY IN A HATEFUL WAY.

Whether in person, on social media, or even through the grapevine, Jesus did not die on a cross so that you could claim to love him yet reflect an opposite result to others (1 John 4:20).

3. JESUS DIDN'T DIE SO THAT WE COULD PURSUE MONEY, FAME, AND MATERIALISM.

The cross points us to Christ, not creation. The gift of grace wasn't presented so that we could become infatuated by the pursuit of riches, titles, and glory. The cross of Christ gives us a new hope, a new vision, and a new purpose—beyond all that. We are called to be "not of this world." As a Christian, your life should reflect an image of grace and selflessness, not greed and self-entitlement (Romans 12:2).

4. JESUS DIDN'T DIE SO THAT WE COULD WEAR CROSSES AROUND OUR NECKS HONORING THE SACRIFICE THAT WAS MADE ON ONE.

A cross isn't just a fashion accessory. The significance of the cross has more weight than any other symbol in the world. And while many use this symbol as nothing more than a piece of bling, God highlights it as the very thing he sent his son Jesus to die upon (1 Corinthians 1:18).

5. JESUS DIDN'T DIE SO THAT WE COULD MAKE MONEY OFF HIS NAME.

Biblically, there is nothing wrong with having a Christian company. The problem is when one uses the name of Jesus to strictly make a profit, with no vision of expanding the reach of his hope. It all comes down to one's motives (2 Corinthians 2:17).

6. JESUS DIDN'T DIE SO THAT WE COULD LIVE A LIFE FREE FROM PAIN.

Free from pain? Nope. But with strength to lean on during trials? Yes. Becoming a Christian doesn't mean that life will be just peachy, but it does mean you will have someone to rely on during times of pain and suffering (Matthew 11:28).

PRACTICE WHAT YOU PREACH

Let's take a moment to ask some questions.

1. Am I a poser?
2. Do I claim one thing but live another?
3. Am I much different than the Pharisees?

As I sit here in my local coffee shop and drink my overpriced iced vanilla latte (a real manly drink), I've begun looking around me wondering what kind of lifestyle I am portraying. I'm sure it has nothing to do with my skinny-jeans and pierced ears, but instead the two open Bibles on my table.

I've noticed a few people walk through the entrance and stare, dumbfounded and confused, as if I was doing something too radical to be seen in public. One lady even gave me a little *pffff*, rolled her eyes, and then made her way to the nearest barista to get her caffeine fix. As much as I try to fight them, insecure thoughts have now begun running through my head. *Maybe I should put my*

*Bibles away so I don't make people feel uncomfortable.
Or, Maybe I should go to a different coffee shop where the
tables are a little more private.*

But a few seconds later I've snapped out of my trance
of insecurity and said to myself, *No! This is exactly why
I am writing this book. So people who claim to love Jesus
will start acting like it, regardless of who or what they
are surrounded by.* As silly as the title of this book may
sound, I want to make sure that my life portrays a living, breathing, love-wearing, grace-pouring example of
Christ. That's not just confidence: it's Jesus swagger.

It's time to stop making up excuses about why we
can't be what God has made us to be. We should care less
about the coffee shop lady's shallow opinions, and only
focus on the one that matters: God's. And since the day
I was born, God set aside a place for me in his kingdom,
just as he has for you. Our calling is to walk like Jesus
walked, talk like he talked, and serve like he served.

As I continue to write this, there is a battle for my
heart being fought every single day. And it's happening
within you too. No matter where I am writing, tweeting,
preaching, or walking, the world will try to pull me one
way, while the truth of the gospel moves to lead me the
right way. It's a battle that we must prepare for every day
of our lives.

In Revelation 3:16 we see Jesus share his thoughts of what he thinks about posers in the Christian faith. "But since you are like lukewarm water, neither hot nor cold, I will spit you out of my mouth!"

The word *spit* in Greek is *ekptuó*, which literally means "spit out, disdain, reject, or loathe."[7] In other words, Jesus despises the posers of Christianity so much that you could say it makes him gag. You don't need to have a theological degree to understand that's probably not a good thing.

But while Jesus weeps over the posers of the Christian faith, so many of us live our lives as if it's okay. Let's call it *purposeful ignorance*. That's when you know what you are engaging in is wrong, but you pretend to be ignorant toward the morally correct answer in order to justify engaging in it anyway. I firmly believe that the closer we get to God, the farther away from lukewarm living we will be.

This type of committed lifestyle doesn't just happen overnight. We must ask ourselves where our roots are truly planted, and make a decision to get away from lukewarm faith. In Scripture we can find Jesus sharing a relevant parable to better equip the crowd before him to do just this. One of my favorite readings on this parable is found in *The Message*, where it's titled "The Story of the Seeds."

As they went from town to town, a lot of people joined in and traveled along. He addressed them, using this story: "A farmer went out to sow his seed. Some of it fell on the road; it was tramped down and the birds ate it. Other seed fell in the gravel; it sprouted, but withered because it didn't have good roots. Other seed fell in the weeds; the weeds grew with it and strangled it. Other seed fell in rich earth and produced a bumper crop. (Luke 8:4–8 MSG)

Imagine a dramatic pause here before Jesus goes on.

"Are you listening to this? Really listening?"

His disciples asked, "Why did you tell this story?"

He said, "You've been given insight into God's kingdom—you know how it works. There are others who need stories. But even with stories some of them aren't going to get it:

Their eyes are open but don't see a thing,

Their ears are open but don't hear a thing." (Luke 8:8–10 MSG)

Here Jesus screeches to a halt and actually explains his own parable. He doesn't look for another creative illustration or explain with another story, as he did so many other times. He just spells it out to his followers. That's how important it is.

"This story is about some of those people. The seed is the Word of God. The seeds on the road are those who hear the Word, but no sooner do they hear it than the Devil snatches it from them so they won't believe and be saved.

"The seeds in the gravel are those who hear with enthusiasm, but the enthusiasm doesn't go very deep. It's only another fad, and the moment there's trouble it's gone.

"And the seed that fell in the weeds—well, these are the ones who hear, but then the seed is crowded out and nothing comes of it as they go about their lives worrying about tomorrow, making money, and having fun.

"But the seed in the good earth—these are the good-hearts who seize the Word and hold on no matter what, sticking with it until there's a harvest." (Luke 8:11–15 MSG)

These words cut to the core of what it means to have mediocre faith, and they tell us what attributes are necessary to a faith that is unshakable. The elegant words of Jesus give a clear understanding to all who are willing to digest their importance. If you are looking to grow, widen, and produce a relationship with Jesus that is unshakable, then why would you plant yourself anywhere that lacks the proper soil and nutrients? In a dry desert without any fellow Christians or people to pray with you? In a self-centered existence where you don't sacrifice lovingly for anyone? In a frenetic, busy life that leaves no space for hearing God's voice?

No matter where the seeds of your life have fallen, you must come to see that God is always willing to replant you whenever you are ready. No past, present, or future is broken enough to be kept from the all-consuming grace of God. Let your faith shine bright, and let your roots be planted in the enriched soil of God's will.

I can't help but thank God for being more than gracious enough to replant me amid several different instances throughout my life. I pretended to know him as a child, and purposely ignored him during my teenage years. Spiritually, I was all over the place. I did whatever I could to make people happy. It wasn't until I was around twenty years old that he finally yanked me up by my roots, replanted me, and became my everything. Although I didn't deserve to be given a second, third, and fourth chance, God continued to show his unending grace and fiercely convicted me of what changes needed to be made in order to fully experience the life he had planned for me.

I realized how far I had traveled away from God's direction, and it was only in my dark and haunting loneliness that I realized how badly I truly needed him. I thought I could do things on my own while juggling a relationship with God that was good enough, to at least pass as acceptable. I needed help. I needed to focus my heart's desires on his name, his love, and his promises. I needed to get closer to my Creator.

FIVE WAYS TO GET CLOSER TO GOD

1. ADMIT YOU CAN'T DO EVERYTHING ON YOUR OWN.

One of the first steps to gaining a closer relationship to God is admitting that you need him in your life. Here's the truth. We can't do everything on our own, so admitting this will not only drive home a sense of humility, but also will show God that you have faith in his strength and promises.

2. REMOVE YOURSELF FROM HARMFUL RELATIONSHIPS.

One of the biggest roadblocks to finding a deeper relationship with God is a harmful relationship. Whether with family, friends, or coworkers, taking yourself out of the equation will help give you the space and energy needed to first get right in your relationship with God. Although this might sound tough to accomplish, you won't believe the freedom and liberty you will encounter when you are able to focus solely on your relationship with God.

3. GET PLUGGED INTO A LOCAL CHURCH OR SMALL GROUP.

You won't believe how much having a group of people to support you will encourage you along your journey with God. Getting plugged into a local church or small group will help keep you accountable, give you wisdom when needed, and even provide for you in times of distress. The church of God was intended to operate in community, so I encourage you to find a community that cares about your relationship with God as much as you do.

4. READ YOUR BIBLE ON A DAILY BASIS.

Reading your Bible is key. You don't need to memorize the whole thing in Greek, but you should be spending time reading it at least once a day. Whether you simply read it, listen to a podcast, or go through a devotional, reading your Bible will help build a foundation for your faith in God. Write down notes that you can look back to, and always be transparent when incorporating what you've learned. God will speak to you in ways that will not only transform you from the inside out, but will give you a better grasp of who you are.

5. MAKE PRAYER A PRIORITY.

Prayer is key. Although prayer can sometimes feel weird or awkward in the beginning, it really doesn't have to be. In fact, it can be incredibly fun. Look at prayer as a conversation between you and God. You don't need to light candles, burn incense, or even wear a black robe. Just relax, get somewhere peaceful, and begin a conversation with God that will help build your relationship with him. Martin Luther once said, "You cannot find a Christian who does not pray to God; just as you cannot find a living person without blood."[8] That quote is packed with powerful truth, and I want you to begin looking at prayer as your way of staying connected to God. Any relationship with meaning is one that has great communication.

SIX WAYS TO HAVE A LUKEWARM RELATIONSHIP WITH GOD

1. ONLY VIEW GOD AS YOUR TICKET OUT OF HELL.

God is more than a get-out-of-hell-free card, and our relationship with him should reflect something much deeper than that. Heaven isn't a place for people who fear hell, but instead a place for people who passionately love God. Don't make your relationship with God transactional. He's worth more than anything your mind can fathom. He's not here just to be personal fire insurance. A relationship with God is something to marvel over. It's a relationship unlike anything this world can offer you.

2. ONLY PRAY WHEN YOU NEED SOMETHING.

Have you noticed that everyone seems to pray when things get tough? The real question is whether or not you are going to extend your prayer life beyond the hard times. God is looking for a relationship with you, and only by communicating with him will you be able to deepen and nourish it. Take prayer as an opportunity to connect with God daily. This time of one-on-one communication will not only help you grow spiritually, but it will nourish your personal relationship with God.

3. ONLY READ YOUR BIBLE DURING A CHURCH GATHERING.

If you want a relationship with God, then I suggest you read the Word he breathed into life. Read a devotional, join a Bible study, or even read the Bible from beginning to end. Regardless of how you read your Bible, God is looking for you to open up his Word and digest the wisdom he has prepared for you. Let's just get real for a moment: There is no such thing as a Christian who ignores God's Word.

4. ONLY WORSHIP DURING A CHURCH SERVICE.

Worshiping during church service is great, but worshiping outside of that element is even greater. Find ways to worship God throughout your everyday life, and make a priority out of giving praise to the One who created you. Worshiping God can be done through many different forms—music, prayer, art, and anything that moves your soul. So find a way to praise God that reflects who God created you to be.

5. ONLY GIVE BACK WHEN YOU GET SOMETHING IN RETURN.

True giving means expecting nothing in return. Whether you are giving to a charity, a church, or even a mission trip, if you are only doing it because it's tax refundable, or because God might bless you for blessing others, you might want to question whether or not your heart is in the right place.

6. ONLY CLAIM TO BE A CHRISTIAN WHEN IT BENEFITS YOU.

Anyone can claim to be a Christian when things are easy. The real question is whether or not you will represent your faith in times of trial and tribulation. Right now there are people all around the world being martyred for their faith, and many of us won't even claim our faith because we're afraid people might make fun of us. Ouch. Is your love for God worth giving everything up for? Is it a privilege and a joy that is stronger even than the fear of death?

≋

No matter where you have fallen in the soil of God's garden, I would encourage you to truly evaluate yourself in a way that strives for deeper roots and widened branches. God is looking for people who are truly committed to his cause, his mission, and his love.

There are plenty of ways to have a lukewarm relationship with God, but there is only one way to have a thriving one with him: pursue him. It's all about commitment and the pursuit of God's love. A fully committed follower of Christ will never find himself or herself lacking guidance or purpose.

CHAPTER 3

LOVE WITHOUT LIMITS

I can't ever recall a person who came to know
Jesus because of hate. #JesusSwagger

Do you ever question whether or not you are good enough to be a Christian, or holy enough to be loved by God? Well, here are four things God's love won't hold against you.

1. YOUR PAST

Relax. You have already been forgiven. When it comes to a relationship with Jesus, don't ever expect to run into resentment from Christ himself. The future looks bright for all those willing to walk in the light of his presence. Jesus will forgive you of your past, even if you have yet to forgive yourself.

> We know that our old self was crucified with him in order that the body of sin might be brought to nothing, so that we would no longer be enslaved to sin. (Romans 6:6 ESV)

2. YOUR MISTAKES

We've all made mistakes, but the beauty of the cross is that Jesus died for them. Your sins have been wiped clean, and your heart has been renewed by the grace of Jesus himself. Your mistakes do not define you. Your failures don't have to haunt you. Your mishaps don't need to be accounted for. God forgives you for your mistakes, even if you have yet to forgive yourself.

> Truly, I say to you, all sins will be forgiven the children of man, and whatever blasphemies they utter. (Mark 3:28 ESV)

3. YOUR CONFUSION

It's okay to be hurt, confused, and question what's taking place. God understands everything you are going through, even if you do not. He can take the punches, if you will take the time to seek his guidance. The reality of your confusion may be due to a lack of biblical knowledge or spiritual guidance. Confusion comes and goes, but the love of God is eternal.

> For the LORD gives wisdom; from his mouth come knowledge and understanding. (Proverbs 2:6 NIV)

4. YOUR ADDICTIONS

Everyone is addicted to something. No matter if your struggle is drugs, alcohol, sex, pornography, or whatever, your addictions will not keep the relentless love of Jesus from embracing you. Take a deep breath and find peace in knowing that you are not alone or ignored.

> Now the law came in to increase the trespass, but where sin increased, grace abounded all the more. (Romans 5:20 ESV)

~~~

God's love for you is stronger than the darkness of your past. The beauty of God's love is that it is relentless, ongoing, undaunted, and never failing. What else in this world can offer you that? Nothing. The cool thing is, we get to showcase this same relentless love to those around us.

Romans 3:23–26 shows us a breath of God's relentless love, one that overpowers any mistake or failure we can ever make. His grace not only brings us a forgiveness we do not deserve, but continues to provide understanding in the lives of all who call Jesus their Lord.

> For all have sinned and fall short of the glory of God, and are justified by his grace as a gift, through the

redemption that is in Christ Jesus, whom God put forward as a propitiation by his blood, to be received by faith. This was to show God's righteousness, because in his divine forbearance he had passed over former sins. It was to show his righteousness at the present time, so that he might be just and the justifier of the one who has faith in Jesus. (Romans 3:23–26 ESV)

The meaning of this verse is simple: God will love you no matter the circumstance.

Can you say that you reflect the same image to others? Do you love without limits? Do you love without boundaries? Do you love without conditions? I'm already asking myself the same questions, evaluating what I've said or done today, and whether or not my life is truly lived with relentless love.

Jesus' love has always been a mystery to me. It's something that my mind cannot fathom fully, nor can I comprehend it spiritually. And although I know his love is without hesitation, it blows my mind to see the beauty of it in action and his pursuit of those he calls "his children."

A WEE LITTLE LOVE

The story of Zacchaeus is one many people can remember hearing in the early days of Sunday school. I can remember the coloring books, cartoons, and Velcro picture boards, all about how Jesus showed love to a "wee little man" named Zacchaeus. The kicker in this story is not just that Jesus showed him love, but that it was given to him before there was any sign of repentance for his wrongdoings.

Zacchaeus was a tax collector who took advantage of those he was collecting from. Not only did Zacchaeus take money from those less fortunate, but when sending the taxes he collected to the Romans, he was known for keeping some for himself.

He was a rich man with a small stature and no friends. Zacchaeus's love for money was apparently what kept him from seeing his need for the love of Christ. Then one day, while Zacchaeus was walking through the town of Jericho, he saw a vibrant crowd coming his way. Because there had been so much chatter about Jesus, my guess is that Zacchaeus hoped it could be the one who called himself the Son of God—the man who was giving sight to the blind, healing the sick, and the man who came to seek and save the lost.

> Jesus entered Jericho and was passing through. A man was there by the name of Zacchaeus; he was a chief tax collector and was wealthy. He wanted to see who Jesus was, but because he was short he could not see over the crowd. So he ran ahead and climbed a sycamore-fig tree to see him, since Jesus was coming that way. (Luke 19:1–4 NIV)

After Zacchaeus climbed a sycamore-fig tree, I can only imagine how excited and nervous he must have been as he sat in that tree waiting for a glimpse of Christ himself.

> When Jesus reached the spot, he looked up and said to him, "Zacchaeus, come down immediately. I must stay at your house today." So he came down at once and welcomed him gladly.
>
> All the people saw this and began to mutter, "He has gone to be the guest of a sinner."
>
> But Zacchaeus stood up and said to the Lord, "Look, Lord! Here and now I give half of my possessions to the poor, and if I have cheated anybody out of anything, I will pay back four times the amount."
>
> Jesus said to him, "Today salvation has come to this house, because this man, too, is a son of Abraham. For the Son of Man came to seek and to save the lost." (Luke 19:5–10 NIV)

Did this really just happen? Did the blunt and boorish tax collector just get asked to host Jesus himself? As the crowds looked upon what had just taken place, I can't help but think all of them were baffled. To think that the selfish and surly tax collector was just befriended by the man who claimed to be the Son of God. Any preexisting idea of who Jesus was, was just thrown out the window when he made this misfit move. I love Jesus for this because he was always surprising people in the way he did things. It's almost as if he was saying, "You don't know me the way you think you do."

Looking at the inner workings of this story, I notice how powerful and life changing it is for anyone who thinks he or she is not worthy enough to receive the love and compassion of Jesus. In a single action, Jesus showcased to all who were watching that his love does not have boundaries, no matter the depth of one's wrongdoings.

There are millions of other people in this world who are living a life outside the image of Christ, but still find their curiosity leading them up a tree in hopes of getting even the smallest glimpse of him. Their lives may not make them out to be someone who deserves his love, but just as Jesus stated in Luke 19:10, "For the Son of Man came to seek and to save the lost" (NIV).

Your past failures and mistakes are irrelevant to the all-consuming love of Christ. We are all lost, broken, and in need of divine love. The story of Zacchaeus is an eye-opener to say the least. And while not everyone will be able to understand the works of God, this doesn't mean that love given through Jesus and his Holy Spirit is at all lacking. What we cannot see, God still provides. What we cannot understand, God still creates. And what we cannot comprehend, God still continues to make reality.

You may be a lot more like Zacchaeus than you think. Or you may know someone who needs love just as much as he did. No matter what side of the gate you're on, the ideology of love is the same.

Notice that after Zacchaeus accepted the offer to befriend Jesus and host him at his household, his entire mind-set and posture was radically changed. Zacchaeus went from a money-hungry punk to a selfless and loving man whose heart was yearning to make right the corruption that had hurt all those around him.

It's amazing how a single act of love can transform someone from the inside out. Even in your life, one single act of love could be the tipping point to someone knowing the truth of Christ, so don't withhold that from anyone you come across. In the same way that Jesus was willing to show love to a man who most would say didn't deserve it, you and I should be willing to go to great lengths to show love to people all around the world.

Whether you think you are qualified or not, Jesus will pave the way if you are simply willing. Sometimes your willingness to love those who need it will be the difference maker in whether or not people come to realize the love of Jesus really does exist.

LET THERE BE LOVE!

It's sad to sit back and watch the media cover nothing but the faults and failures of proclaimed "Christ-followers," instead of getting down to the truth of what 98 percent of us do differently than the 2 percent who make us look bad. If the negativity that the media portrays is in fact the world's view of what it means to be a Christian, please don't call me one. I'd rather call myself a Christ-follower than be thrown into the twisted view of what we've made "Christians" out to be. I understand that *Christian* actually means *Christ-follower*, but you get where I'm going with this.

The word *Christian* has become too common over the years. Not for the sake of spreading the good news of Jesus, like we'd hope for, but instead that of comfort and ease. People say "I'm a Christian" as easily as they would "I like hamburgers."

For many reasons, the word *Christian* has stopped being associated with the word *love*. It's stopped being associated with grace. This isn't a matter of theology, doctrine, or philosophy, but instead of the actions people take—or don't take—in the name of Christ. Jesus called us to love one another as he has loved us (John 13:34). Simple. This means we are to relentlessly, passionately, and fervently love one another just as he has loved us, *no matter the circumstance*. But does this really happen?

The ideology of "hate the sin, not the sinner" has *not* converted well into today's culture. If you take a moment to look around, you'll notice that we are very good at showing hate to the people whom God has called us to love. Regardless of what the Bible says about cursing, drinking, homosexuality, sex, cheating, lying, or stealing, we are still called *to love one another*. It's that simple. No questions asked, regardless of how you interpret Scripture.

Does this frustrate anyone the way it frustrates me? And before you say anything about seeking to keep your brother or sister accountable, please remember that you and I both sin as much as the next person. The goal isn't to look away when someone is struggling, but instead to engage and embrace people in a way that reflects the loving comfort of Christ. A way that shows the love of Jesus. A way that turns from anything to do with hate. Period.

"Hate the sin, not the sinner" isn't working. Honestly, I don't believe it ever has. When hating the sins of others, people just simply don't know how to separate the sinner from the sin. I encourage you to instead "Love the sinner, not the sin." Remove the word *hate* from your vocabulary, and start reflecting an image of Jesus that portrays him differently than a man standing on a soapbox wielding a megaphone. I can't ever recall a person who came to faith because of hate. Let's start a movement of people who are willing to take hate out of the equation and love people regardless of their sins.

When Jesus called us to love one another, it wasn't limited by guidelines or parameters. The commandment was simple and to the point: "A new command I give you: Love one another. As I have loved you, so you must love one another. By this everyone will know that you are my disciples, if you love one another" (John 13:34–35 NIV).

There are no regulations on who and when to love. Love is not ours to control, monitor, and divvy up. Love was never intended to be kept to ourselves. It was meant to be shared with anyone and everyone willing to accept it.

The idea of loving without limits may seem a little intimidating, but that's the raw beauty of it. Sometimes loving people might not make sense, but it still makes a difference.

I remember hearing a story from my friend Mike Foster of a man named Emmanuel, who was part of the Rwanda genocide in 1994. As part of the Hutu majority, he assisted in the killings of nearly a million people, and one of those people was the husband of a Tutsi woman. Emmanuel later came to find shame in his actions, and he then asked for the forgiveness of the man's wife. Not only did she express that God had already forgiven him for his actions, but that she did as well.

What reckless love was shown through the actions of this woman. Where the rest of the world might give her an excuse to eternally hate this man, she instead harnessed the love of God and offered a place of forgiveness and grace.

If anyone should be leading the way for love and compassion, it should be the followers of Love himself—Jesus. When we begin to view people through the eyes of Jesus, we are less likely to see their flaws and more likely to see their need for love.

All throughout Scripture we see Jesus loving people whom others deemed foul, broken, dirty, and unworthy. To us that may mean the homeless drunk guy, the prostitute hanging out downtown, the person in jail, the drug addict—even the convicted sex offender. People may criticize you for giving your time and attention to people who are ostracized or considered permanently broken. They may say it's not safe, that they're not worth your time, and that these people gave up the right to be treated well when they made their bad decisions. They said that to Jesus too. But while many self-proclaimed followers of God sat back and criticized the openness of Jesus' love for people, he called them out for their lack of it:

> And as he passed by, he saw Levi the son of Alphaeus sitting at the tax booth, and he said to him, "Follow me." And he rose and followed him. And as he reclined at table in his house, many tax collectors and sinners were reclining with Jesus and his disciples, for there were many who followed him.
>
> And the scribes of the Pharisees, when they saw that he was eating with sinners and tax collectors, said to his disciples, "Why does he eat with tax collectors and sinners?" (Mark 2:14–16 ESV)

Take notice that even the Pharisees and other religious leaders are confused as to why Jesus is extending love to those who are sinners, tax collectors, prostitutes, and thieves. The love Jesus showed to these people was without boundaries or regulation. He was giving it all to people who might not even recognize him as the Son of God. The beauty of this is that Jesus knew these people couldn't offer him anything in return, and yet he still embraced their friendship and presence.

Jesus' response to the religious elite was nothing short of jaw-dropping: "And when Jesus heard it, he said to them, 'Those who are well have no need of a physician, but those who are sick. I came not to call the righteous, but sinners'" (Mark 2:17 ESV).

The sick, or the sinners, were the people who needed the most urgent shot of love. You probably have someone in mind right now who could be classified as one of "those who are sick." Hey, it may even be you. But no matter the person or their beliefs, when you show them love, you show them the Spirit of Jesus himself.

DISPENSABLE LOVE

Recently I was hiking through the trails of Washington State on a beautiful Sunday afternoon. Whether I am hiking the mountains, fishing the streams, or simply looking for an adventure, getting outdoors and into the wild is something I've always loved to do. There is a spiritual awakening that comes with adventuring through God's creation. Although the weather in Washington can get pretty cold, it's easy to build up a sweat while trekking through the rugged wilderness, especially while wearing a few layers of clothing.

I'm an avid watcher of those reality survival shows, so I absolutely love the idea of being in the woods, having to survive on my own, and protecting myself from the dangers of the wilderness. A friend of mine had recently given me a survival kit for Christmas, so I was pretty excited to try out some of the items that came along with it. I'm not sure if he gave it to me as a joke or not, but I was all for using the kit in a real-life situation—even if it was just for a day.

I'd probably actually enjoy getting lost in the wild and having to rely on a small kit like this—but let's be honest. I also love learning everything I can as I watch from the comfort of my living room, eating popcorn instead of worms and bugs and whatnot.

On my walk, as I continued traveling down the bank of a river, I noticed that my water bottle was looking a little empty and I had nothing left to drink in my backpack. Instead of chancing the salmon-crowded river water below me, I decided to make my way back toward a little town I had spotted when I parked my car. I must not have been as far into the woods as I thought, and to my surprise it only took me about fifteen minutes to get where I was headed.

I walked up to the local park and tried getting a water bottle out of the vending machine. To my surprise there was no water in stock, and I was out of luck. I took a moment to examine my surroundings, and I realized that this little town was in fact abandoned, and not the lively place I hoped it to be. I took a few minutes to walk about the area, in hopes of finding a small convenience store. Once again, I was out of luck and without water.

I decided I was going to have to try my luck with the stream water, but I was hesitant knowing I could get extremely sick. Why? Because it was spawning season, and the last thing you want to do is drink water where salmon are spawning. I don't need to further explain, do I? Yuck.

Just as I was about to make the plunge in drinking the river water, I heard a voice in the distance. To my surprise, a man with his dog came out of the woods, jogging with an overnight backpack on. I gave him a quick wave and he ran over to me with a smile on his face. I kindly introduced myself and then asked if he knew of anywhere I could get some water. He looked around and said, "Here, there are some cabins just over that hill. Use one of their community fountains." He pulled a small trail map out of his backpack, circled a specific location, and then handed it over to me with a huge smile on his face. "Really?" I asked. He nodded his head and went back to running. Before I could say anything else, he was up the hill and back on course to his adventure.

It took me another ten minutes to find the cabins he was talking about, but man, were they a sight for sore eyes. I walked up to the community water fountain, filled up my water bottle, and found myself extremely relieved.

I sat down, drank enough to get myself rehydrated, and then made my way back to my car, grateful that I'd avoided heatstroke. I can't begin to explain how refreshing and rejuvenating that water was.

That afternoon, the fact that I could easily and freely access water from that fountain stuck with me. God's love is also described as a fountain of "living water" that is always available to us in our driest times (John 4:10). The thing is, if God is the water, then we should be the ones sharing his love. We dispense his love to those who need it. It's our calling. A drinking fountain isn't going to judge how much you drink, what you did in your past, or whether or not you deserve a sip. It's simply there to refresh and rehydrate you in your time of need. Aren't we called to do the same thing to people all around the world?

Imagine if everyone who called him- or herself a Christian loved like a water fountain. No matter who needed love, why they needed it, or whether or not they deserved it, love would be poured out with nothing asked for in return. Think about how many community water fountains there are in this world. Imagine if all of those were actually people standing by and giving love to anyone who crossed their path. How would our society be different?

Mind you, we all can't stand around and just wait for someone in need. But we can take time out of our busy schedules to stop and pause for a moment when it's needed, and to put others before our calendars.

A JOYFUL DEBT

We are called to love like this for a very good reason: because Christ first loved us. He paid for our sins on the cross. That puts us in a sort of joyful debt to him—where we live a life of gratefulness, freedom, and love in return. While earthly debt is destructive, the debt of love is life-giving. Paul says in his letter to the Romans, "Let no debt remain outstanding, except the continuing debt to love one another" (13:8 NIV). What does this mean? Origen wrote in the second century, "Paul wants every debt of sin to be paid and absolutely no debt of sin to remain among us, but for our debt of love to abide and never cease; for paying this debt even daily and owing it at all times is beneficial to us."[9]

The Christian is always a love debtor, no matter how much love he gives. If you have ever had a personal debt, be it ever so small, you know that the first thing that enters your mind when you see that person is that you "owe" them. It may be nerve-racking, but that urgency makes us spring to action. Being a spiritual debtor is much less nerve-racking, but the sense of positive urgency remains. When we go to church, town, work, shopping, school—wherever we go, whoever we meet, we owe love. As R. Kent Hughes says, "This is our debt—loving on the level."[10]

When it comes to loving people, let's not allow it to be something we do on the side. Let's make it part of who we are. Let's make it a lifestyle. Whether we are at the gas station, picking up groceries, even waiting to get our car repaired, there is always an open opportunity to love someone in need.

Having been able to preach all across the United States in the last few years, I came to realize that no matter where I am located, people are always in need of love. Whether I was in the rainy streets of Seattle, on the border of Mexico in Laredo, Texas, or all the way across the country on the sandy beaches of Florida, it's all the same. Love is a language that's relevant in all cultures.

LOVE IS A VERB

Have you noticed that people use the same word to explain their affection toward chocolate as they do to their husband or wife? How frivolously we use the word *love*.

A bar of chocolate and a wife are two completely different things that deserve two completely different descriptions. To me, that shows that we need to deepen our conversation about what love really means.

Today's concept of love seems to be extremely shallow.

And while I know not everyone may speak and think of love frivolously, I would bet that the general population would agree we need to do better at it. According to a 2011 census, 41 percent of all marriages in the United States now lead to divorce.[11] Why such a shocking figure? It might have something to do with the way we use the word *love* as a noun, rather than a verb. So many people think of it as a "thing" instead of an "action."

Although my wife and I still have many years ahead of us, it doesn't change the reality that we need to constantly pursue one another's hearts. No matter how long you've been with someone, this fact doesn't change. Utilizing love as a verb in our relationship has completely transformed the way we see each other. Not only do we affirm each other by saying that we love each other, but we show our affections through actions and follow-through. A hug here, a kiss there, a sacrificial act of service, a gift, a listening ear, a frank talk, a fun night out—love in action makes a huge impact over time. The only way it works is if we take each day as an opportunity to relentlessly pursue one another.

But there is an example far greater than what we humans can do for one another. It's the transcendent act of love that God showed on the cross through Jesus. Words fail us when it comes to describing the cross. Because of that ultimate loving act, we're called to pursue a lot less talk and a lot more action. Not only are we to exhibit love through our everyday actions, but we are to be a living exhibit of Christ's love. It's a lifestyle that can only be shown through experiencing a life in Christ.

LOVE LIKE A SAINT

When I think of radical, unlimited love, I immediately begin to think of a humble woman who has become an icon of grace and selflessness: Mother Teresa. Not only was this woman a bold and vibrant example of the love of Jesus, but she relentlessly showed love to the "least of these"—the lepers of Calcutta (Matthew 5:19). In some of her most famous words, she drives home an amazing point: "You may be exhausted with work, you may even kill yourself, but unless your work is interwoven with love, it is useless. To work without love is slavery."[12]

I wish I could have met this woman before she passed away, because her story and testimony have completely changed my life for the better. Other than Jesus himself, Mother Teresa is hands-down one of my favorite historical world changers. Her story is one that provides an exuberant example of how Christ will provide for those who are willing and open to God's work. Here is how one of her biographers described her beginnings:

Named Agnes Gonxha Bojaxhiu, Teresa was born an Albanian in Skopje, Yugoslavia. Her father was a prominent businessman and her mother a helper of the poor. As early as age twelve, Teresa saw herself as a devout Catholic with missionary interest in India. In 1928, on graduating from high school, she joined the Sisters of Loretto, an Irish order of missionary nuns. After a year's study of English in Ireland, she arrived in Calcutta, India, in 1929.

Two years later, vows of poverty, chastity, and obedience concluded her novitiate. She took her name from Teresa de Lisieux, who emphasized joy in menial tasks. In 1937, she became Mother Teresa through further vows. From 1931 to 1948, Teresa taught geography and history at St. Mary's School, her order's high school in Calcutta. But by 1946, she believed God had given her another special call: to live among and assist Calcutta's most desperate poor.

Mother Teresa secured permission to begin her new ministry in 1948. After a year's training as a nurse, she founded a school in one of Calcutta's slums. Before long, she had attracted numbers of dedicated workers. In 1950, the Vatican approved organization of her work as the Missionaries of Charity. A fourth vow became basic to this group: wholehearted free service to the poor. As her efforts proceeded, Teresa was appalled at some of the slums' hideous conditions. Consequently, she resolved to concentrate on the worst of the diseased and destitute. With her various helpers, she approached Calcutta's most afflicted lepers, trash-disposed infants, starving families, and beggars—the deformed and helpless of all ages and backgrounds.

Thus, among other facilities, Teresa's Calcutta work eventually included a home for the dying, an orphanage, a leper colony, an employment workshop, various medical centers, and countless shelters. But soon Calcutta could not contain Teresa's vision. In 1965, she was permitted to extend her ministries to other parts of the world. By 1986 the Missionaries of Charity had founded centers in Venezuela, Ceylon, Tanzania, Rome, Cuba, and other locations. These all implemented Teresa's call to the "poorest of the poor" . . .

In 1979, she accepted the Nobel Peace Prize. Overruling critics, the Nobel Committee stated that she made efforts for peace by her "confirmation of the inviolability of human dignity." In the name of "the hungry, the naked, the homeless," Teresa accepted all prizes, using any monetary awards toward purchasing more facilities. Above all, in describing her motives, she spoke of Christ's love and his commands to respect each human life. . . . About her ministries, she claims to have done no great things, only small tasks in the power of Jesus's love.[13]

As I sit and ponder the life of Mother Teresa, I can't help but envision a woman who, without fear, let nothing stop her from sharing the love of God. No brokenness, no disease could keep her from helping the people she was called to shower in love. She didn't have any limitations on love. Her passion and purpose to love kept her heart focused on the ideology to "love because he first loved us" (1 John 4:19 NIV).

Mother Teresa was a rare breed of human—a love-sharing juggernaut—but that same beautiful truth is also a saddening truth. Why is it so rare? It makes me think about my motives for sharing love in my own life. I constantly question whether or not I am loving in a way that reflects the true being of Jesus, or whether my actions are merely motivated by the good feeling I get after handing a homeless man some change. Is sharing love in a limited capacity just another way of being a poser Christian?

My wife and I have learned that our calling in life isn't to make ourselves feel good by helping others, but to relentlessly help others regardless of whether it's convenient for our personal lives. This means things like pulling over on the freeway to help a family with a flat tire, bringing lunch to a homeless man down the road, or helping a mother bring all of her groceries to the car. Loving others isn't about us at all. And until that sinks in, we'll never be able to love the way Christ truly loved.

Mother Teresa selflessly put aside her personal needs, wants, and comforts in order to love those whom society rejected. While the rest of the world overlooked the diseased people of Calcutta, Mother Teresa loved them relentlessly, passionately, and without limitation. It might be bizarre to imagine Mother Teresa walking the streets of India with Jesus swagger, but she embodies the second key to swagger so well: loving with sacrifice, as God did, and accepting God's love yourself. This led her to confidently stride into areas of disease and suffering, knowing that God would protect her, uphold her, and make her a fountain of mercy. May we keep her in mind as we swagger on.

CHAPTER 4

CHURCH WITHOUT WALLS

"You can't be a church without
a building," said Jesus, never.
#JesusSwagger

≈

I was visiting a new church for the first time since relocating for a new job. I had heard nothing but great things about this church from the people around me, so I figured we would give it a shot since I was looking for a new place to call home. As I drove up to the building I noticed it was smaller than I had expected, but that didn't really matter since my goal was to find community rather than get lost in a crowd. And while my previous experiences in the church had already given me preconceived notions about what our experience might be like, the Spirit reminded me that not all churches are the same, and that my old ways can't get in the way of what God might do through me today.

As I walked in to find my seat I could already tell I was out of place. I was probably the youngest person in the congregation, and everyone around me either had four kids or was starting to get some grey hair. This doesn't mean that God couldn't have used this church to speak to me, but the reality was I was looking to build community with people my age and in my stage of life.

Ignoring the age difference of the people around me, I went through the motions of a typical church service. I listened to the announcements, awkwardly tried to sing a few songs I didn't know, and then got up to greet people around me before the pastor was scheduled to come up and teach. I'm dead serious when I say I stuck out like a sore thumb. I'm positive people thought I was someone's grandkid visiting for the weekend, partially because I looked like I was sixteen, and partially because I was a third of the age of everyone attending.

As I returned to my seat, the pastor took his place in the pulpit and began preaching a message that started like most, but eventually he said something that has forever opened my eyes. It wasn't the message itself that tore me apart, but what was happening to the right of me in the church foyer that brought me to tears and ignited a bomb of righteous frustration.

The message was dedicated to how the congregation was to rapidly grow over the next few years, how they planned on expanding their building, how they would accomplish reaching thousands of new members, and in what ways they could make the experience of attending their church better. He proceeded to go off on a tirade about how their congregation needed to work more with the homeless, help hurting families, and be there for the least of these (Matthew 25:40). It was one of those tirades that every communicator, including myself, goes on when they are fired up about something. And while he continued to passionately preach to his congregation, my eyes glanced toward a group of individuals with stringy hair, dirty clothes, and tattered jackets sitting on chairs in the lobby across from my seat. *What are the odds of that?* I asked myself.

I immediately thought, *You should go see if any of them want to sit with you.* I got up from my chair and walked over to a man who seemed as if he was in deep thought, and unaware of his surroundings. I introduced myself and asked for his name. "Roger," he said, as his toothless smile lit up the entire lobby. I asked if any of them would like to sit with me during service, and his response to me is what has forever changed my view on the church.

"We have to stay right here," he said with a timid voice, as one of the staff members looked on at both of us with crossed arms and a tough grin. In my confusion I asked him again, hoping that I had just heard him wrong. But as he repeated exactly what I had thought he said, my anger toward the church staff began to grow, and I assured him it would be fine if he and some of his pals sat next to me. Glancing nervously at the two staff members now crowding us, he insisted on remaining in the lobby in hopes of staying out of trouble. They were sitting in a small and separate seating group reserved strictly for homeless individuals. And with a handshake and exchange of names I stumbled back to my seat with a disgruntled expression on my face while the staff members looked at me like I was some sort of crazy person. As service ended and people began getting up from their seats, I watched dozens of people walk past Roger and his friends, not even giving them a glance. As most of the congregation flooded out of the building, Roger and his pals were then asked to grab their stuff and told the service was now over. I can't imagine what Roger must have been feeling, but everyone in the congregation acted as if he and the rest of his group were invisible.

I find myself in tears as I think about how humiliated and rejected Roger must have felt while being ignored by a church, and put in a corner like a dog needing to stay out of trouble. I don't know his entire life story, but I can only imagine the circumstances that brought him to where he is today are anything but glamorous and joyful.

To this day I still wish I would have left my seat and sat with Roger and his group in the lobby, but I'm assuming my frustrations kept me from thinking straight, or maybe it was that I was still working through my time as a poser Christian. The rest of the service that day I couldn't concentrate; I kept asking God, *How could anyone let this happen? Isn't this supposed to be a church?* and *Didn't the pastor just get done saying how we need to help the hurting?*

At that moment I realized how backward the purpose of churches has become. We've become so infatuated with bringing people into our buildings, making them extremely comfortable, and verbally designing an idea of what we think Christianity is supposed to look like, that we have forgotten that the very message of Jesus was to "go and make disciples of all the nations" (Matthew 28:19). Including our own—and the hurting people in them.

I'm not ignorant enough to believe that every church in the world would act the same way this one did, but I will say that this experience opened my eyes to something many churches in the world are at fault for. We lack the boldness to reach outside of ourselves, and we're afraid to get the carpets dirty. We look more like museums than we do biblical churches.

From the very foundations of the Bible, we find examples of the church reaching outside of itself, meeting people where they are, and going to great lengths in order to help those who are in need. The church was never intended to be exclusive, but so many of us have turned our ideology of its purpose into a club that meets once a week in a building made by man. The church was never meant to be a members-only country club.

Are church buildings wrong? Of course not! They are a wonderful tool that can be utilized to host gatherings, provide shelter, and even create a 24-7 communal space for those in need. But when the sole focus of a church becomes "How many people we can bring inside our building?" we've completely missed the mark. We can't expect to create an influx of hope in our culture while we continue to close the church doors behind us.

CHURCH AND CASINOS

Over the last few years God has given me the wonderful opportunity to visit and preach at some incredible churches. And while every church has its own strengths and weaknesses, there are always a few churches that stand out to me more than most.

The last place anyone would expect to see a thriving church would be the city of Las Vegas. But while many people deem this fast-paced entertainment capital "Sin City," my dear friend Jud Wilhite has other plans for this community. Jud is currently the pastor of a church in Las Vegas, a place he has decided to call Grace City. And while many people in the world may scarcely hear about the struggles of porn, drugs, prostitution, gambling, and other addictions in their congregations, this is something Jud and his staff see on a daily basis.

Jud's church reminds me of a quote I once read by Abigail Van Buren: "Church is a hospital for sinners, not a museum for saints."[14]

I've actually heard their church once described as one big AA meeting. And if you really think about it, that's a huge compliment! I believe Jesus would applaud that. If you remember, Jesus himself spent time with sinners, prostitutes, drunks, and swindlers (Luke 15:2). He was always showing affection to those who the world would overlook.

And while it would probably be fairly easy for Jud and

his staff to ignore the pain and suffering coming through their church doors, they instead open themselves up to anyone and everyone who is looking for help. They aren't afraid to get their carpets dirty, deal with some tough issues, and reach outside their comfort zone in order to benefit a person in need of God's love. Trust me, I've seen it firsthand.

Their team has people who are constantly reaching out to local bars, casinos, and strip clubs, all in the hopes of bringing people to Christ. Not to judge or condemn, but to love and offer help for addictions they might not even know they have. I'm not telling you to barge into your local strip club, bar, or casino and proclaim the name of Jesus. But I am telling you that God is using some incredibly willing people to reach the ones no one else is reaching, by doing things no one else is doing.

I'll never forget the first time I ever visited Vegas. Jud's executive staff picked me up from the airport and then took me to lunch. I wasn't too sure where we were going to eat, but they told me they had something special in store for my arrival. To my surprise, we ended up at a buffet, in a casino, on the Las Vegas strip. *I hope nobody tells my mother about this*, I thought to myself. I find it kind of funny that my first trip to Vegas was to visit a church, rather than all the things that city has to offer. And if you think that's crazy, what's even crazier is that the staff told me not to be surprised if some of the people who attended or even served at their church were currently working at that very casino.

"We come here to show people we aren't above or beyond them," they told me. "You'd be surprised to know how many people who are working the tables are also serving with us on Sunday mornings."

I was blown away by the church's willingness to break down the walls and barriers of its congregation, and open itself up to the entire city of Vegas. It's no wonder this church is one of the biggest and fastest growing churches in America. They're extending the same love, grace, and hope that Jesus himself did. There are no limitations or boundaries as to who was handed a hearty helping of church. Sin City better look out.

As the lunch conversation continued on, I couldn't help but remember what Paul stated in 1 Corinthians 9:22–23:

> When I am with those who are weak, I share their weakness, for I want to bring the weak to Christ. Yes, I try to find common ground with everyone, doing everything I can to save some. I do everything to spread the Good News and share in its blessings.

What a beautiful example of a church without walls. Pastors, staff, elders, and an entire congregation who are willing to step outside of their comfort zones and meet people where they are.

If that wasn't enough already, the church also has specialized meetings for just about anything you can think of. Single moms, prison inmates, drug addictions, domestic abuse, victims of rape or child abuse, individuals with disabilities, and more. They have opened their arms to anyone and everyone in need of love, grace, and a second chance.

Mind you, this church doesn't claim to be perfect. In fact, they don't even claim to be almost perfect. But the beauty behind what this church team is doing in Vegas is their willingness to show relentless love to people all across their city. In the same way, I believe all of us need to strive for this very thing. No matter who you come across, where you meet them, or where they are in life, you and I can always be open and willing to be the church.

THE EARLY CHURCH

The Greek word for church is *ekklésia*, which means "assembly." You can find the first use of this word in the New Testament when it is spoken by Jesus in the book of Matthew. Jesus stated to his disciples, "I will build my church" (16:18). This assembly was built upon his character and power, and it was never meant to be done in any other way.

After Jesus said this, he began meeting with people around the tabernacle, and later the temple. Although Jesus used the tabernacle and temple as meeting places, kind of like we do, the foundation and purpose of the church is found in him alone—and not the meeting place in which it is being held.

Most would say that the beginning of the church can be found in chapter 2 of Acts, where the disciples had been overcome by the work of the Holy Spirit and were equipped for their evangelistic mission (vv. 1–4). That church's existence testified to the resurrection of Jesus, which began a new age for believers and still affects the world around us.

Immediately after the disciples shared their teachings, a church of community and fellowship was born. The communities were filled with acts of prayer, the sharing of bread, and worship. The early church was founded on the aspect of community and how one could help the needs of others. There was no official building to meet in, but the church of Jesus grew still: "praising God and enjoying the favor of all the people. And the Lord added to their number daily those who were being saved" (Acts 2:47 NIV).

Many scholars and theologians would claim that this model of church would not last in today's society, but when it comes to people who are looking for biblical community, I'd bet differently. There is a hunger for community, and it doesn't matter where it meets—be it a shopping center, bar, movie theater, home, park bench, or stained-glass cathedral. A buildingless community is definitely not the only way to be the "authentic" church, but it's an intriguing option.

When I begin to evaluate what people are actually looking for in a church setting, nine times out of ten I will get a response that has to do with finding a community of people to do life with. If this is the case, then I can't see why an Acts 2 model of a deepened sense of community and founded on the power of the Holy Spirit would not work.

The church that propelled me into my ministerial journey was one in Corona, California, called Crossroads Christian Church. And at the age of twenty I dedicated my life to the Lord, got baptized, and immersed myself into a life of ministry. Not only did God provide me with incredible leaders, but the mission and purpose of the church was summed up into three words that I believe are the crux of our faith: *Christ, cause,* and *community.* These three words not only helped mold the church's vision, but also kept it focused on God's purpose for the congregation.

I started off like everyone does in ministry. I was an intern who basically did what I was told, walked in a posture of learning, and allowed myself to be molded and poured into by the leaders around me. I learned how to serve. Even in my first few years of ministry I noticed a theme in those around me: a yearning for community. People were excited for events, concerts, and special guests at the church, but for some reason nothing compared to everyone's desire for biblical community in the daily rhythm of their lives.

Yes, the church had a vision for growth and expansion; but they placed extreme emphasis on the act of building community outside of the church's walls. Even after being away for quite some time, I can see that the church's mission and purpose remains the same, and the leadership continues to make strides to expand their "outside-the-building" communal efforts. They are meeting in lower income neighborhoods, with after-school programs and a day-care center, and it's really changing their community. Other than service on Sundays and a student gathering on Mondays, every group or meeting of people meets outside of the church, immersed in the surrounding community.

No, that church is not perfect. But yes, it's effective in reaching people who aren't already part of a church. We won't ever be able to duplicate an exact match of the Acts 2 church, but God does give us the wisdom and guidance necessary to get pretty dang close.

Don't get me wrong. I understand that culture and society are way different than they once were, but we need to remember that Jesus is still the same. He is the same today as he was yesterday and will be tomorrow (Hebrews 13:8). We can't limit what the church is capable of due to a time and date. When we embrace the power of the Holy Spirit, we can reach outside the walls we have built around us.

I have nothing against church buildings, but I do have something against how they make people view the church's purpose. We sometimes use the walls around us as a comfort and safety zone. It's as if we've tricked ourselves into thinking the church only exists when we are within a certain parameter, and ends once we step outside and get into our cars.

The *ekklésia*, or church Scripture talks about, is living, breathing, and organically built by the Spirit of God. Yes, we can bring our own unique visions and style into the mix, but to think we can fully control a community that was meant to be guided by the Spirit is heretical. As Charles Wood said,

> A lovely building is not a church. All the beams, joists, decking, pews, seats, pulpit furniture, carpet, fixtures, woodwork, organ, piano, speaker system, chalkboards, easels, and podiums do not make a church. These merely form a church building or the building where the church meets.[15]

Some say that no church building is actually ever mentioned in the New Testament. Instead people met and "broke bread" within the comfort of their homes (Acts 2:46 NIV).

This doesn't make a church building wrong, but it does make it nonessential. To think that we cannot praise, worship, serve, or proclaim the love of Jesus without four walls and a pulpit is false beyond measure. The church is people. We are the church (Matthew 18:20).

KNOW YOUR NEIGHBORS

The second is equally important: "Love your neighbor as yourself." No other commandment is greater than these.

MARK 12:31

Do you know your neighbors? Every day we run across people who are working at gas stations, flipping burgers, working at nail salons, and wiping down tables. Imagine if we all took a second out of our day to learn their names, ask how we can pray for them, and intentionally make it a point to come back and see them again. Now, you might be thinking, *That's kind of weird and overbearing.* But it's actually reflecting a vibrant image of Jesus Christ.

So, yes—it is weird, if by *weird* you mean *different*. As Christ-followers, we are called to be different from the rest of the world and to love people without limits. That's surely something this world isn't used to. In the same way we show love to our friends, family, and coworkers, we need to be extending that same love and compassion to the people we come across casually in our everyday lives. At one point in time, every friend was a stranger. Love changed that.

This type of love will only work if it is intentional, selfless, and nontransactional. In order for us to begin a lifestyle of love, we must be intentional about giving it. It will blow you away to see how the most unlikely of people can become the closest of friends, all through the act of intentional love.

What's the difference between *being* the church and simply inviting people to one? It's showing relentless love. This will let us see every place, from the gas station to the grocery store, with an entirely new set of eyes. Before we love, though, we must get to know people. Knowing your neighbor is slowly becoming a faded concept, perhaps because while many people in this world truly yearn for the love and affection friendship brings, many of us are putting our own agendas before the needs of others. We are pulling through the drive-through in a hurry to get to work, rather than sharing a kind word. We are brushing by people on our way to somewhere else "urgent," and maybe even getting too attached to our "me time."

When we put others before ourselves, we are directly telling them that we love and value their lives. This might mean taking time out of your busy schedule to stop and let someone know how much you appreciate his or her hard work, or even paying for the coffee of the person behind you. For some people, this might be exactly what they needed to keep from giving up, quitting the job they feel unappreciated at, or even endangering their own lives. So next time you have to make a decision between keeping things running smoothly with your day or showing love, try showing it, and see what a difference it makes.

CHAPTER 5

JESUS ISN'T HIRING PART-TIME DISCIPLES

Everyone is called to
full-time ministry, no matter
where you live or work.
#JesusSwagger

Here's a little questionnaire for you.

1. Do you call yourself a Christian?
2. Do you believe in the power of God's Word?
3. Do you believe the Bible is the inerrant and inspired Word of God?

If you answered *yes* to these questions, congratulations: You've just applied yourself for a life of full-time ministry.

You might think,

But I don't work at a church . . .

But I don't work for a Christian company . . .

But I don't have time to serve in ministry . . .

If you claim to be a Christian, then the question of "the meaning of life" is already solved for you! The purpose of your life is to share the redemptive qualities of Christ (Matthew 28:19). You *are* in the ministry.

Galatians 2:20 reads, "I have been crucified with Christ; and it is no longer I who live, but Christ lives in me; and the life which I now live in the flesh I live by faith in the Son of God, who loved me and gave Himself up for me" (NASB). There is vital truth to what this verse states. It is no longer *you* who lives, but Christ who lives *in* you. Meaning, it's no longer about your agenda, your desires, and your needs. If you call yourself a Christian, your agenda is now filled with an all-consuming calling from Christ himself.

That hits me pretty hard. All the selfish desires that you and I have should now be thrown out the window, and all focus trained on Jesus.

Your current situation and workplace are your personal mission field. Why? Because you can reach people a church can't. You're on the front lines! You might even have a better opportunity to reach people than a missionary or church professional does. Don't let anyone tell you that full-time ministry can only be found within the confines of a church building. God is bigger than four walls and a steeple.

God has put the people around you in your life for a reason. Find out what that reason is, and make it your mission to empower their lives with Christ. Jesus will always supply you with the necessary tools and weapons needed to conquer anything that comes in your path.

Work at a grocery store? Perfect. You have the opportunity to share and reflect the love and servanthood of

Christ to dozens of customers a day. Work for a restaurant? Awesome! Use your time at work to share your testimony with your coworkers, or even share a reflection of Jesus' kindness to each person who walks through your doors. If you really look, there are endless possibilities for anyone who is looking to be a full-time disciple of Jesus Christ.

Your job title doesn't matter, but the way you use your time does. Stop letting people tell you that working for the government or for your company isn't God's plan for you. Stop allowing the opinions of man to keep you from being a light to your current workplace (Matthew 5:14). Just because you may not have a seminary degree and a position serving in a local congregation doesn't mean you're not in full-time ministry.

Jesus himself wasn't paid by a church. He was a carpenter who used his everyday knowledge of work and carpentry to relate to the people he was surrounded by. Yes, men like Paul and Peter dropped everything to follow the plans of Jesus, but don't forget about the thousands of other people who stayed where they were in order to be a light where it was needed.

The New Testament couple Priscilla and Aquila are perfect examples of this. Acts 18:2–3 tells us:

> [Paul] became acquainted with a Jew named Aquila, born in Pontus, who had recently arrived from Italy with his wife, Priscilla. They had left Italy when

Claudius Caesar deported all Jews from Rome. Paul lived and worked with them, for they were tentmakers just as he was.

We can see that both Priscilla and Aquila were tent makers who helped Paul on his missionary journey by allowing him to live and work with them in order to provide for himself. Their regular work flowed seamlessly into their ministry—a ministry that happened to help during one of the most critical points in Christian history. Tent makers, yes, but history makers too.

Step out and start vocalizing what God has put on your heart. If you're not willing to do it where you are, what makes you think you would do it somewhere else?

When we think about work or vocation, there's always the issue of money—of getting paid for what you do. It's tempting to put earning a living before being in ministry where you are ("I need to focus on surviving before I focus on other people"), but God's logic is the opposite. I know people who make less than $15,000 a year and have thriving ministries. I also know people who make well over six figures a year and can't seem to find their ministerial fit. Your paycheck, job title, and spare time are irrelevant factors to whether or not God can use you. He looks at your heart, not your bank account. And he can use you right now. You have the option to change the world starting with the people who are standing right in front of you. If you don't reach out to them, who will? I wouldn't leave that up to chance, or give up the opportunity to make an unprecedented ripple effect on the world around you. The potential is limitless.

The ideology of every Christian embracing a lifestyle of full-time ministry has the potential to transform the world from the inside out. It's a possibility that could truly reach the far ends of the world for the sake of the Gospel. Imagine if everyday people, working everyday jobs, meeting everyday customers, all shared the extraordinary salvation given through Jesus Christ. The potential is limitless.

My sister is a perfect example of someone who is using her current situation in life to better serve the church of Jesus. And while my sister isn't on staff at a church, nonprofit, or any other Christian-based ministry, that hasn't stopped her from going on four missionary trips to Africa, serving at the local shelters on a weekly basis, and striving to help extinguish the global sex trafficking trade, all while attending school full time and working as a waitress. Yeah, she's pretty awesome.

And don't even get me started on my wife. This woman lived on her own for years before we were married and has worked full-time jobs since she was seventeen, all while serving more than forty hours a week at local ministries. Not to mention that she has spent an extended amount of time serving in Honduras to help with a privately run orphanage. Why, you ask? Because she has a passion and purpose in the Lord that all people who call themselves Christians have access to. She started serving with what she had, and it snowballed into something beautiful. Her willingness has opened the door for her to change so many lives in the name of Christ. She uses her everyday experiences as an opportunity to change someone's life, no matter the scenario.

In order to embrace the true Jesus swagger lifestyle, embrace the mission of using every moment available to share your faith in Christ. There are no limitations on where God can work.

Let me say it again: Jesus isn't hiring part-time disciples. While this may discourage you in the beginning, I would encourage you to allow it to fuel your purpose in life. Stop, take a deep breath, and make today the day you start using every avenue available in every place, no matter how mundane, as a way to share the hope, grace, and salvation of Jesus Christ. Trust me, it's worth every moment.

RECLAIMING CULTURE

"Christians are so narrow-minded" is a phrase I hear almost daily. And while much of me thinks that's entirely false, I can't help but question if that's the reality for most. While many people in this world do their best to stay away from what the evangelical crowd might call "secular" life, I tend to be the person who pushes firm believers into the center of it in order to make a difference. Call me unconventional.

I'm not proposing that you should frequent the local party scene, get drunk with your friends, post scandalous photos on your social media channels, or become infatuated with money and material things. Of course not. But what's stopping you from being the one to make a difference in the secular world? What's wrong with showing an example in dark places? If you won't, who will?

Honestly, I think many of us are just too scared to jump headfirst into something Christian culture calls "secular." That word sounds scary. And while I agree there are many things one should stay away from as a Christ-follower, there is a mature and honorable way to go about being a Christian while still being engaged in today's culture. Once again, Christ called us to reach "all the nations," not just Christian cliques (Matthew 28:19).

I believe Jesus came to reclaim culture, not reject it. We talk so much about wanting to change the world for Jesus, but in the same breath we tell people not to engage in the culture surrounding us. Jesus called us to change the world from the inside out, and that begins with us equipping ourselves to evaluate culture, engage culture, and then reclaim the culture for the teachings of Jesus.

Whether it is the job you take, the music you listen to, the movies you watch, or the way you dress, there is always a way to reflect an image of Christ no matter the circumstance. Just because some might not understand it doesn't mean it's not right. I can't begin to tell you how many times I've been criticized for the way I dress, or the fact that my ears are pierced, the way I have decided to cut my hair, or that I decided to get a tattoo of a cross on my chest when I was eighteen. These are all things that others might look at and deem unbiblical, but I tend to look at each of them as biblically redeemed. These are things one can choose to do in a way that glorifies Christ.

God has called us to reclaim the world he created for his name and purpose. There are many things in this world that culture has used for darkness, but in reality can and should be taken back in the name of Christ. Music, visual art, and the entertainment industry are all examples of arenas we can seek to reclaim for the sake of Jesus. Don't let culture be what changes your relationship with God. *Do* feel free to let your relationship with God help you change and contribute positively to culture.

PREACHING WITHOUT A PULPIT

The idea of preaching without a pulpit might seem a little crazy to some, evoking images of shouty people standing on street corners, waving Bibles at pedestrians. But the concept of pulpitless preaching is not so narrow. In fact, it's one of the callings God has placed on each of our lives. Not only are we all called to share the gospel with the nations, but also we are called to do it in a fearless way: "Since this new way gives us such confidence, we can be very bold" (2 Corinthians 3:12).

I receive messages and e-mails from people from all around the world asking for evangelistic advice. People who want help sharing Jesus with their friends, family, and strangers. And while I always find it easy to give advice to those who need it, I am constantly asking myself if I am listening to the same advice I am giving. If you were to ask yourself when the last time you shared Jesus with someone was, what would the answer be? That answer will tell you a lot about your relationship with him.

I love seeing teenagers who are fired up for Jesus sharing his story with people at malls, schools, and grocery stores. Many of today's youth have more audacity and boldness than those who claim to be mature believers in Christ. That change in living may be derived from "growing up," and being told to chill out over the years, but I believe this is something we need to evaluate and change our view on. We can keep that radical way of living in our hearts. We can keep living an audacious life in the name of Jesus. We're called to be radical. There is no other way to live the Christian life.

In the same way I see youth groups and Christian clubs excited to use the people around them as personal mission fields, I would hope to see my generation and beyond be passionate for the same thing.

So why do so many of us hold on to the idea that we need a church building, or some sort of official sanction to preach the Word of God? There are many events in the Bible where Jesus preaches to the masses. Not in a church building, temple, or religious organization, but in the open for all to hear. Jesus constantly used his surroundings as a platform to share truth and religious liberation. One of the most classic examples of this is described in the book of Matthew. The story goes, "One day as he saw the crowds gathering, Jesus went up on the mountainside and sat down. His disciples gathered around him, and he began to teach them" (5:1–2). No pulpit. No ushers. No printed bulletins. Jesus saw the people, and dug in for the long haul. He must have looked around and seen the faces of hundreds of people who were hurting—who needed hope. And he reacted with a set of teachings we now call the Sermon on the Mount. It's one of the most intense streams of wisdom in the Bible. All from a dusty hillside in Judea.

THE SERMON ON THE MOUNT

Jesus said to the people:

> God blesses those who are poor and realize their need
>> for him,
>> for the Kingdom of Heaven is theirs.
> God blesses those who mourn,
>> for they will be comforted.
> God blesses those who are humble,
>> for they will inherit the whole earth.
> God blesses those who hunger and thirst for justice,

for they will be satisfied.
God blesses those who are merciful,
  for they will be shown mercy.
God blesses those whose hearts are pure,
  for they will see God.
God blesses those who work for peace,
  for they will be called the children of God.
God blesses those who are persecuted for doing right,
  for the Kingdom of Heaven is theirs.

God blesses you when people mock you and per-secute you and lie about you and say all sorts of evil things against you because you are my followers. Be happy about it! Be very glad! For a great reward awaits you in heaven. And remember, the ancient prophets were persecuted in the same way. (Matthew 5:3–12)

For those in the crowd who were poor and in rags, for those who mourned, and those who were ostracized and mocked for following Jesus, this must have been like a cool drink of water. Same for us. How many other people over the ages must this have inspired to be humble, to hunger for justice, to show mercy, and to have a pure heart?

But Jesus saw more opportunity for encouragement.

Have you ever silently noticed someone, and regret-ted not telling them what potential you saw in them? When you got great service, saw someone do something you admired, or even loved the way a dad was interacting with his kid? Jesus wasn't about to let the opportunity go to waste. He knew that each person could be a beacon, and he didn't shy away from telling it to them straight, looking in their eyes, and calling out their potential for his kingdom—right there on the hillside.

TEACHING ABOUT SALT AND LIGHT

You are the salt of the earth. But what good is salt if it has lost its flavor? Can you make it salty again? It will be thrown out and trampled underfoot as worthless.

You are the light of the world—like a city on a hilltop that cannot be hidden. No one lights a lamp and then puts it under a basket. Instead, a lamp is placed on a stand, where it gives light to everyone in the house. In the same way, let your good deeds shine out for all to see, so that everyone will praise your heavenly Father. (Matthew 5:13–16)

Then it was time to get down to some things we might gloss over in polite conversation. This is a heavy dose of truth-telling, arranged in a "you may have heard this, but I tell you something completely different" manner. He even begins, "Don't misunderstand . . ."

How many times have you seen misconceptions about our faith and thought to yourself, *They're not even trying to understand what it really means!* Or, *I just really don't want to get into this with this guy right now.* Here in this famous street sermon, though, Jesus shows us how to straight-shoot, confronting misconceptions about our faith head-on. After all, in light of eternity, what's the use of letting them slide in order to avoid an awkward moment?

Jesus cared about these people, and he needed them to know the truth—that what they had "heard said" was not reality. This part of the sermon covers some sensitive stuff: the law, anger, adultery, revenge, giving, prayer, judging, consequences, heaven and hell, and pretty much the real grit of humanity's deepest issues. But he does it without mincing any words, and while still showing love.

TEACHING ABOUT THE LAW

Don't misunderstand why I have come. I did not come to abolish the law of Moses or the writings of the prophets. No, I came to accomplish their purpose. . . . So if you ignore the least commandment and teach others to do the same, you will be called the least in the Kingdom of Heaven. But anyone who obeys God's laws and teaches them will be called great in the Kingdom of Heaven. (Matthew 5:17–19)

Here he calls for responsibility. There's no hint of "follow God's laws because they'll make you happy and give you your 'best life now.'" There's no "just maybe give it a try if you're comfortable with it." Instead there's an acknowledgement of the pure, all-encompassing rightness of God's commandments, and how critical they are to the foundation of a righteous life.

TEACHING ABOUT ANGER

You have heard that our ancestors were told, "You must not murder. If you commit murder, you are subject to judgment." But I say, if you are even angry with someone, you are subject to judgment! If you call someone an idiot, you are in danger of being brought before the court. And if you curse someone, you are in danger of the fires of hell. (Matthew 5:21–22)

Contrary to the world's way of riding the anger train wherever it leads us (into court? into a yelling fight in the parking lot? into sabotage, slander, or worse?), Jesus gives us the option to get off at the first stop. We can all see the practical application of this; Jesus makes it a spiritual one too.

TEACHING ABOUT ADULTERY

You have heard the commandment that says, "You must not commit adultery." But I say, anyone who even looks at a woman with lust has already committed adultery with her in his heart. So if your eye—even your good eye—causes you to lust, gouge it out and throw it away. It is better for you to lose one part of your body than for your whole body to be thrown into hell. (Matthew 5:27–29)

Again, tough words. But with refreshing, cleansing power, purifying power. Jesus probably wasn't expecting the people to start hacking away at themselves in the crowd, but he knew how to convey to them the importance of intentions, and how small beginnings grow into great tragedies. Again, a blend of practical and spiritual.

TEACHING ABOUT DIVORCE

You have heard the law that says, "A man can divorce his wife by merely giving her a written notice of divorce." But I say that a man who divorces his wife, unless she has been unfaithful, causes her to commit adultery. And anyone who marries a divorced woman also commits adultery. (Matthew 5:31–32)

TEACHING ABOUT VOWS

You have also heard that our ancestors were told, "You must not break your vows; you must carry out the vows you make to the LORD." But I say, do not make any vows! . . . Just say a simple, "Yes, I will," or "No, I won't." Anything beyond this is from the evil one. (Matthew 5:33–37)

In a world where divorce is all around us, where vows are broken every day, this teaching is no more popular than it was then. There are countless hearts wounded, hurting, and crying out for healing because of divorce and the pain that it causes. This is not something to be taken lightly, and Jesus thought so enough to devote these lines to it in his sermon.

TEACHING ABOUT REVENGE

You have heard the law that says the punishment must match the injury: "An eye for an eye, and a tooth for a tooth." But I say, do not resist an evil person! If someone slaps you on the right cheek, offer the other cheek also. . . .

You have heard the law that says, "Love your neighbor" and hate your enemy. But I say, love your enemies! Pray for those who persecute you! In that way, you will be acting as true children of your Father in heaven. . . . If you are kind only to your friends, how are you different from anyone else? Even pagans do that. But you are to be perfect, even as your Father in heaven is perfect. (Matthew 5:38–48)

Jesus reminds us here about the greatness of God. God doesn't need to fight for his rights with us, or to force us to comply. He gives and gives, grace upon grace, without ever running out. What would the world look like if we did the same?

TEACHING ABOUT GIVING TO THE NEEDY

Watch out! Don't do your good deeds publicly, to be admired by others, for you will lose the reward from your Father in heaven. When you give to someone in need, don't do as the hypocrites do—blowing trumpets in the synagogues and streets to call attention to their acts of charity! I tell you the truth, they have received all the reward they will ever get. But when you give to someone in need, don't let your left hand know what your right hand is doing. Give your gifts in private, and your Father, who sees everything, will reward you. (Matthew 6:1–4)

The crowd on the hillside already knew they were supposed to give to the needy. That's not the revelation here. What they needed to hear was that God cared about *why* they did such things. God sees down deep to each atom of our makeup, each tiny thought, each breath, each feeling, and wants to soak it in righteousness. If you do a right thing for your own glory, you've just killed it. The action may be complete, but no love comes of it. God is not honored. You look like a chump. God looks at us, all striving and performing and running like hamsters in wheels, and wants to tell us to stop what we're doing, look at our hearts, accept his love, and then try again with new energy straight from his endless supply.

TEACHING ABOUT MONEY AND POSSESSIONS

Don't store up treasures here on earth, where moths eat them and rust destroys them, and where thieves break in and steal. Store your treasures in heaven, where moths and rust cannot destroy, and thieves do not break in and steal. Wherever your treasure is, there the desires of your heart will also be. . . . No one can serve two masters. For you will hate one and love the other; you will be devoted to one and despise the other. You cannot serve both God and money. . . .

So don't worry about these things, saying, "What will we eat? What will we drink? What will we wear?" . . . your heavenly Father already knows all your needs. Seek the Kingdom of God above all else, and live righteously, and he will give you everything you need. So don't worry about tomorrow, for tomorrow will bring its own worries. Today's trouble is enough for today. (Matthew 6:19–34)

So should you scrap your 401(k)? Hold a massive garage sale? Start passing out your Benjamins on the street? Hey, if you are up for getting radical, I'm not going to stop you. But what I think Jesus is aiming at here is our *hope*—what we place our hope in. If our savings go bust and our houses burn down, will we despair and lose complete hope in life? Will we completely give up, thinking back on all the hours, relationships, and opportunities we sacrificed just to get all that "stuff" that is now gone? Or will we let God set the value on the things in our lives? The "treasures in heaven" he's talking about have the amazing side effect of giving us peace of heart here on earth.

DO NOT JUDGE OTHERS

Do not judge others, and you will not be judged. For you will be treated as you treat others. The standard you use in judging is the standard by which you will be judged.

And why worry about a speck in your friend's eye when you have a log in your own? How can you think of saying to your friend, "Let me help you get rid of that speck in your eye," when you can't see past the log in your own eye? Hypocrite! First get rid of the log in your own eye; then you will see well enough to deal with the speck in your friend's eye. (Matthew 7:1–5)

Here's something we recovering posers need like cold water to the face. Comparing ourselves to others (and subsequently judging them) is our stock in trade. These planks in our eyes are huge, but we've decorated them with blinging cross ornaments and Christmas tree lights. But there's a better (and less tacky) way to live. When we let Jesus do the eye surgery, it's a whole lot easier to get around, and we can enjoy others instead of judging.

EFFECTIVE PRAYER

Keep on asking, and you will receive what you ask for. Keep on seeking, and you will find. Keep on knocking, and the door will be opened to you. For everyone who asks, receives. Everyone who seeks, finds. And to everyone who knocks, the door will be opened. (Matthew 7:7–8)

Jesus has told us a lot about what *not* to do at this point. But here he gives the crowd a power boost: We don't have to fix ourselves. We don't have to figure it out from scratch. God is waiting to help us.

THE GOLDEN RULE

Do to others whatever you would like them to do to you. This is the essence of all that is taught in the law and the prophets. (Matthew 7:12)

TRUE DISCIPLES

Not everyone who calls out to me, "Lord! Lord!" will enter the Kingdom of Heaven. Only those who actually do the will of my Father in heaven will enter. On judgment day many will say to me, "Lord! Lord! We prophesied in your name and cast out demons in your name and performed many miracles in your name." But I will reply, "I never knew you. Get away from me, you who break God's laws." (Matthew 7: 21–23)

Motivation, motivation, motivation. Jesus is obsessed with your motivations. He cares that you feel connected personally to what you "do unto others." He cares if you are posing as someone who calls him "Lord! Lord!" but never actually took the time to know him at all.

Authenticity counts so much that it's a deal breaker. And when the crowd on the hillside heard him preaching, they could tell that he had it pouring from within him.

BUILDING ON A SOLID FOUNDATION

Anyone who listens to my teaching and follows it is wise, like a person who builds a house on solid rock. Though the rain comes in torrents and the floodwaters rise and the winds beat against that house, it won't collapse because it is built on bedrock. (Matthew 7:24–25)

Just as one would expect, the crowds were amazed by the teachings of Jesus. Not only because of his knowledge and wisdom, but because "he taught with real authority—quite unlike their teachers of religious law" (Matthew 7:29). He gave them a "solid rock" to build on, where they had been slipping around on the sand. It was the truth, and the first time many had heard it. A total game changer.

None of it would have happened if Jesus had not taken the opportunity to boldly preach where most would not have expected. I believe he gave his disciples something to learn by showing what it means to evangelize and teach the public. He taught with a divine authority, spiritual strength, and truth. He spoke again and again about the heart—about motivation, intention, and inspiration. People today thirst to hear the same thing: authenticity counts. Character counts. The truth (and there is a truth) really matters. They're not floating around in an existence where they're forced to just make do with cultivating an image or posing with the "wisdom" of the world around them. There's more. And you get to tell it to them—with or without a pulpit, in every place you go, with everyone you meet.

No matter where you are, how old you are, or who you are with, Christ will give you the necessary tools to share this truth and understanding.

CHAPTER 6

BE THE CHANGE

Christians are called to be the change the world
is looking for. #JesusSwagger

~~~

The world changed completely with the arrival of Jesus, and ultimately will end with Jesus too. But the real question is, what lies between those two points? In order for positive change to happen now, shouldn't we first make sure we have been changed ourselves?

The fact is, we can't bring positive change to the world if we ourselves have not first been changed. There's a popular saying: "Be the change you wish to see in the world."[16] To us, that means being like Jesus. Throughout Scripture we see that we are called to be like Jesus, we are called to be the difference, and that will make the world look a little bit more like him. As Romans 12:2 says, "Don't copy the behavior and customs of this world, but let God transform you into a new person by changing the way you think. Then you will learn to know God's will for you, which is good and pleasing and perfect."

Until Jesus returns with glorious swagger, we are called to "be the change."

Our world often relies on a sense of comfort and stability; change is the last thing most people want to think about. Research shows millions fear change; it even has a name—*neophobia*, or the fear of new things. Yes, it's a real phobia, and yes, it says a lot about human nature. But the danger is that when we cave to our fear and avoid change, we get so comfortable where we are that we ignore the very new things God has initiated to get us where we are heading in life. Sure, we can all dream of things we'd like to change about the world, about ourselves, but we are scared to be the ones to step out and do it—*be it*. When the excuses "I'm not ready for that" or "I'm just not called to do that" come out of our mouths, that could be a sign of neophobia.

When I was younger I once heard a pastor say, "Partial obedience is disobedience." And while everyone around me began to get up from their chairs, clapping and saying, "Amen!" I quietly sat in my seat. The phrase smacked me across the face and pierced me to the core. It's so true. I mean, if we are truly living like Jesus, then why are we still doing "that" (insert sin here)? Why are we refusing to change our ways, when change is what we need most? We cannot go about our lives half-hearting our walk with God, in hopes that he will give us a full-heart transformation. Since we don't automatically have a nature like Jesus', and constantly have to deal with our human failings, we must accept that to be more like him, we'll have to change.

THE KIND OF CHANGE YOU WANT

What does it even mean to live like Jesus? The phrase "live like Jesus" means so many things, and if we put it into practice, it will cause a change in us of immeasurable depth. Yet so many of us are running around like a chicken with its head cut off, only hoping we are living like him.

C. S. Lewis had this to say:

> To trust Him means, of course, trying to do all that He says. There would be no sense in saying you trusted a person if you would not take His advice. Thus if you have really handed yourself over to Him, it must follow that you are trying to obey Him. But trying in a new way, a less worried way. Not doing these things in order to be saved, but because He has begun to save you already. Not hoping to get to Heaven as a reward for your actions, but inevitably wanting to act in a certain way because a first faint gleam of Heaven is already inside you.[17]

God never intended us to remain the same, but instead to remain faithful—to take his advice. For in remaining faithful, we will not remain the same.

There is incredible hope in this. You can be different than you were. You can break the mold of your family's past. You can be different from what everyone else has labeled you. You are made in God's image, for his will. And no human opinion can get in the way of a God-given destination.

You are a mighty warrior of Christ. It doesn't matter how you grew up. It doesn't matter what you did, or didn't do. It doesn't matter if you've been told "You're too young" or "You're just like your dad." What matters to the world doesn't matter to God. And it's time you connect this very truth to the fabric of your heart.

Stop listening to the foolish lies of this world, and start appreciating and accepting the truth of God's Word and the freedom that comes with it. I'm sure you've encountered flaws, failures, and mistakes in your life. But that doesn't mean you have to put up with them, or that things have to stay that way. In fact, if you consider yourself a follower of Jesus Christ, you are called to overcome those very things. This does not mean you will find perfection, but you will undoubtedly find progression on the path of righteousness.

Just because it's how you grew up, doesn't mean it's how you should stay. With Christ comes renewal and a new way of living.

Scripture confirms this hope:

And I will give you a new heart, and I will put a new spirit in you. I will take out your stony, stubborn heart and give you a tender, responsive heart. (Ezekiel 36:26)

Do not conform to the pattern of this world, but be transformed by the renewing of your mind. Then you will be able to test and approve what God's will is—his good, pleasing and perfect will. (Romans 12:2 NIV)

DON'T CONFORM. BE DIFFERENT.

God hasn't called us to "conform to the pattern of this world, but to be transformed" through the sacrifice of Jesus Christ.

To live for God.

To be changed.

To be different from the world.

So are you living for God? Have you been transformed? Are you living different from the world?

We all make mistakes. We all screw up. We all fall short. But in the core of your heart, do you understand what it means to be a follower of Jesus? And based on your everyday lifestyle, do you reflect that?

I ask myself these questions every day. Self-evaluation can make or break your relationship with God. If we can't admit we need help, we will never gather up the courage to ask for it.

God is looking for progression, not perfection. And you can't find progression unless you have direction. Let God be your compass. Let the way you study, spend time with friends, act in your relationships, and learn be done through the direction of God himself.

Look around you. God has divinely placed you in this very moment, to do something *big* for his kingdom. There is no need to worry about who's watching, or what they might think. The only thing that matters are the people around you who don't know the love of God and the beauty he provides in our brokenness. Don't miss out on this opportunity. And remember, God is with you through all. The right time to do the right thing is right now. "For God has not given us a spirit of fear and timidity, but of power, love, and self-discipline" (2 Timothy 1:7).

When we act upon the direction that Romans 12:2 commands when it tells us not to conform, we are engaging in a lifestyle that Jesus rejoices over. It's easy to follow the crowd, conform to the pressures of this world, and submit to the trends that culture gives us. But we were meant to stand out boldly.

Alice Cooper, famous rock and roller, said, "Drinking beer is easy. Trashing your hotel room is easy. But being a Christian, that's a tough call. That's real rebellion."[18]

THE MISFIT GOSPEL

When thinking of individuals who stood boldly for the sake of the gospel, I begin to think of people like Mother Teresa, Martin Luther King, Jr., Billy Graham, and Dietrich Bonhoeffer.

Not only did these people stand up for their faith in a world that saw their beliefs differently, but they went against the cultural norms, ignoring the potential of negative response.

Let's be real with one another. We all want to be liked, cherished, and appreciated by our peers. But what if I told you that God could not care less about these things? What if I told you that God didn't care how many Facebook friends you have, or how many people follow you on Twitter? And what if I told you that I'm almost positive he doesn't care what your Klout Score is?

What if I told you that God isn't worried about how popular you are? In fact, what if the purpose of the gospel isn't to fit in at all, but to stand out for the sake of Jesus?

The Bible says, "Do not love this world nor the things it offers you, for when you love the world, you do not have the love of the Father in you" (1 John 2:15).

Those twenty-eight words carry some major weight in the life of anyone who calls him- or herself a Christ follower. In fact, the basics of a Christian posture are found in the depth of these words: "Do not love this world." And that includes fame, power, popularity, titles, and materialistic value. If that seems rigid, just remember that Jesus died to free you from sins and the shackles of this world—including all these things. My point is, what are your priorities? Whose words are you more yearning to seek: the world's or God's? And whose approval do you care about more?

With little to no faith in God, I jumped into a kiddy pool of acceptance at a pretty young age, instead of a sea of God's truth. Why? Because it wasn't deep and took little to no personal sacrifice on my end. It was the easy way out. Following the pack seemed a lot easier than breaking away. But little did I know that following these people would soon lead to personal and spiritual failure.

I hadn't realized that since Jesus laid his life down for us, the least we can do is stand for him.

In today's worth-seeking world, being liked and wanted is something we all yearn for. And regardless of whether it comes naturally, it's how our culture forces us to feel—even by advertising popularity.

The world says:

1. "Failure is not an option."—NASA[19]
2. "If you are not first, you're last."—Ricky Bobby[20]
3. "If you're not somebody, you are nobody."—
   Popular saying

But when we begin to look into the depth of Scripture, we'll realize that none of those things are actually true. Literally, none of them.

1. Where NASA says "Failure is not an option,"
   Scripture says, "For everyone has sinned; we all fall
   short of God's glorious standard" (Romans 3:23).
2. Where Ricky Bobby says "If you are not first,
   you're last," Jesus says, "So those who are last now

will be first then, and those who are first will be last" (Matthew 20:16).

3. For everyone that tells you "If you're not somebody, you are nobody," the Bible's clear answer is: "God does not show favoritism" (Romans 2:11).

God has called us to be a city on a hill (Matthew 5:14). To go against the grain. And to be the change for a world that lacks hope.

We talked earlier about Scripture's call to transformation in Romans: "Do not conform to the pattern of this world, but be transformed by the renewing of your mind" (Romans 12:2 NIV). While the ideology of that verse stands pretty clear, you'd be surprised to know how many people actually avoid standing out.

Realizing you don't fit in is a good thing. You weren't made to fit in. You were made to fulfill your calling in Christ. You were made to fit out.

Some of us walk, talk, read, and tweet like the most spiritual people ever to inhabit the earth. But behind the plastic mask we call "Christianity" is often merely personal modification rather than actual heart transformation. We seek more width than actual depth, and this show can only go on for so long.

Before you were even born, you were called to be different. You were given the potential for ultimate swagger.

And although being different might sometimes look lonely or unpopular, you must come to see that no matter the circumstance, God is still with you. Why on earth would we continue to cheat ourselves out of God's love, and try to fill the void with worldly acceptance?

I've been blogging for a while now, and that experience has been undeniable proof that I cannot please everyone in this world. I can't even please all the Christians in this world. My wife always tells me, "You can be the ripest and juiciest peach in the world, and you're still going to have people who don't like peaches." No matter what I say or do, there is always going to be someone who doesn't agree with the way I've constructed things. Don't believe me? Start a blog and see for yourself.

You won't believe the amount of hateful, vulgar, and repulsive comments I get from people on a daily basis. Don't get me wrong. I still get hundreds of comments a day from people who are encouraged and inspired by my writing, but this isn't without the few who are looking to start a quarrel.

For every two hundred comments, there are always about ten to twenty people who seem to have it out for me. It doesn't matter what I say or do, they will always have a way to go against my thoughts and question my intent. At first it really bugged me, but over the last few years my wife and I have learned to laugh it off and use it to fuel us.

For example, we had one person tell us that drinking

Diet Coke was a sin, and instead of wasting our money on canned beverages, we should be spending our money on children in need. Sometimes you just can't win. (But wherever this person is in their quest to fight Diet Coke injustice, I wish him or her well.)

Many people have asked me why I like to discuss touchy subjects on my blog. My only response: "It's what Jesus would do." I don't purposely stir up controversy for the fun of it, but I do purposely talk about the tough stuff in order to bring light to a situation that might be drowning in fear. Look back at the Sermon on the Mount. That thing flipped everything those people once knew upside down. I've come to understand that my purpose on this earth isn't to be loved and cherished by everyone around me. My purpose is to share the love of Jesus, show relentless grace, and always be willing to help my neighbor. Surprisingly enough, not everyone likes that.

If you want to fully embrace the life that Jesus offers, be willing to ignore the opinions of man while you engage in the righteous pursuit of Christ. If you haven't experienced any pushback yet, could it be that you are holding back in your ministry?

When we hide behind smooth words and shallow theology, we are indirectly telling God we are not bold enough to speak the truth. I'll be the first to say I still struggle with this on a daily basis. The second my hand hits the keyboard, there is a battle going on in my head.

One side says, *Make sure to keep anything controversial out of this!* While the other side screams, *Speak the truth, in love, even if it kills you!*

Which one do you think Jesus would choose? I believe he would speak the truth, in love, even if it killed him. And eventually it did.

It would be fairly easy for me to write blog posts and books that have no call to action in them. It would be easy for me to write encouraging words that lack any type of conviction. And it would be easy for me to write ear-tickling paragraphs that lack a call to repentance. But frankly, that's not who God has called us to be.

Evaluate your life, your speech, and your conduct. Do you represent Jesus in a way that reflects timidity, or are you speaking the truth in love, and unshaken by the opinions of others? There is no neutrality in the eyes of Jesus. You and I are required to pick a side, no exceptions.

All the posing that we do in order to gain acceptance from the people around us is the very thing that is keeping us from what our hearts truly desire: God. I want to express to you that worldly approval won't last. The world will never fulfill a heart without Jesus.

You and I are called to be the oddballs, the different ones, the black sheep, and misfits in society, all for the sake of the gospel. Make this the starting point to turn things around. Embrace the courage and strength God has provided you through his son Jesus, and make it your mission to teach the truth of God's Word.

A MAN AGAINST AN ARMY

Dietrich Bonhoeffer is not only an inspiration to Christians everywhere, but he is a godly representation of what it truly means to have Jesus swagger. The guy was a misfit beyond measure, and I encourage you to read the story that forced me to completely reevaluate my life, my calling, and the boldness I claim for Christ.

Although Bonhoeffer is no longer alive today, his relentless journey of proclaiming Christ has touched the hearts of millions. In fact, a recent biography of him, *Bonhoeffer* by Eric Metaxas, was a *New York Times* best seller.

Dietrich Bonhoeffer (Feb. 4, 1906–April 9, 1945) was a pastor, theologian, and active member of the German resistance to Hitler and the Nazis. A photo of Bonhoeffer resisting the Nazi salute is an iconic image that has taken our culture's social media channels by storm. Dietrich can be seen surrounded by thousands of Nazi soldiers where he is the only one going against the grain of his surroundings. This is how one biographer tells his story:

> While the election of Hitler was widely welcomed by the German population, including significant parts of the Church, Bonhoeffer was a firm opponent of Hitler's philosophy. Two days after Hitler's election as chancellor in Jan 1930, Bonhoeffer made a radio broadcast criticizing Hitler, and in particular the

danger of an idolatrous cult of the Fuhrer. His radio broadcast was cut off mid-air.

In April 1933, Bonhoeffer raised his opposition to the persecution of Jews and argued that the Church had a responsibility to act against this kind of policy.

Bonhoeffer sought to organize the protestant Church to firmly reject Nazi ideology from infiltrating the church. This led to a breakaway church, The Confessing Church, which . . . sought to stand in opposition to the Nazi-supported, German Christian movement. . . .

As the Nazi control intensified, in 1937, the Confessing Church seminary was closed down by Himmler. Over the next two years, Bonhoeffer travelled throughout Eastern Germany, conducting seminaries in private for sympathetic students. During this period, Bonhoeffer wrote extensively on subjects of theological interest. This included *The Cost of Discipleship*, a study on the Sermon on the Mount, and argued for greater spiritual discipline and practice to achieve "the costly grace."

"Cheap grace is the grace we bestow on ourselves. Cheap grace is the preaching of forgiveness without requiring repentance, baptism without church discipline, Communion without confession. . . . Cheap grace is grace without discipleship, grace without the cross, grace without Jesus Christ, living and incarnate."

Worried by the fear of being asked to take an oath

to Hitler or be arrested, Bonhoeffer left Germany for the United States in June 1939. After less than two years, he returned to Germany because he felt guilty for seeking sanctuary and not having the courage to practice what he preached. . . .

On his return to Germany, Bonhoeffer was denied the right to speak in public or publish any article. However, he managed to join the Abwehr, the German military intelligence agency. Before his visit to the US, Bonhoeffer had already made contacts with some military officers who were opposed to Hitler. It was within the Abwehr that the strongest opposition to Hitler occurred. Bonhoeffer was aware of various assassination plots to kill Hitler. It was during the darkest hours of the Second World War that he began to question his pacifism, as he saw the need for violent opposition to a regime such as Hitler's.

When Visser't Hooft, the General Secretary of The World Council of Churches, asked him, "What do you pray for in these days?" Bonhoeffer replied "If you want to know the truth, I pray for the defeat of my nation."

Within the cover of the Abwehr, Bonhoeffer served as a messenger for the small German resistance movement . . . [where] efforts were made to help some German Jews escape to neutral Switzerland. It was Bonhoeffer's involvement in this activity, that led to his arrest in April 1943. As the Gestapo sought to take over responsibilities of the Abwehr, they uncovered Bonhoeffer's involvement in escape plans. For a year and a half, Bonhoeffer was imprisoned at Tegel Military prison. Here he continued his writings such as *Ethics*. Helped by sympathetic guards, his writings were smuggled out. After the failed bomb plot of July 20, 1944, Bonhoeffer was moved to the Gestapo's high-security prison, before being transferred to Buchenwald concentration camp and finally Flossenburg concentration camp.

Even during the privations of the concentration camp, Bonhoeffer retained a deep spirituality which was evident to other prisoners. Bonhoeffer continued to minister his fellow prisoners. Payne Best, a fellow inmate and officer of the British Army, wrote this observation of Bonhoeffer.

"Bonhoeffer was different, just quite calm and normal, seemingly perfectly at his ease . . . his soul really shone in the dark desperation of our prison. He was one of the very few men I have ever met to whom God was real and ever close to him."

On April 8, 1945, Bonhoeffer was given a cursory court martial and sentenced to death by hanging. Like many of the conspirators, he was hung by wire, to prolong the death. . . .

Just before his execution, he asked a fellow inmate to relate a message to the Bishop George Bell of

Chichester 'This is the end—for me the beginning of life.' The camp doctor who witnessed the execution of Bonhoeffer later wrote, "I saw Pastor Bonhoeffer . . . kneeling on the floor praying fervently to God. I was most deeply moved by the way this lovable man prayed, so devout and so certain that God heard his prayer. At the place of execution, he again said a short prayer and then climbed the few steps to the gallows, brave and composed. His death ensued after a few seconds. In the almost fifty years that I worked as a doctor, I have hardly ever seen a man die so entirely submissive to the will of God."[21]

As I reread the story of Bonhoeffer, I cannot help but feel pain for what he suffered, but I also find myself cheering for his bold and godly audacity. The man was put into a situation in which most would choose to conform and survive, but he stood his ground even against the all-consuming power of the Nazi regime. How many of us can say we've looked the world in the face and told it we only serve one God? Dietrich Bonhoeffer could.

The strength and tenacity Dietrich walked with was something only the Spirit himself could have provided him. The courage to stay grounded in his faith didn't originate in Bonhoeffer alone, but instead it was God working through and in him.

The iconic picture of Bonhoeffer refusing to partake in the Nazi salute is similar to what I believe all Christians face in today's world. You and I are constantly surrounded by a world of temptation, hate, and vulgar motives. The question is whether or not we are going to conform to what's around us, or instead pursue the purpose God has placed within us.

Bonhoeffer is a man I will always look up to and aspire to be more like. I can't say that I have been faced with the danger he once stood before, but I pray that you and I will also show the same bold posture no matter what we face. Jesus swagger is a relentless, bold, and audacious way of living—one that ignores all opposition in order to live out the life that Christ has called us to live.

CHAPTER 7

I GOT 99 PROBLEMS BUT THE HOLY SPIRIT AIN'T ONE

The Holy Spirit is in the business
of exalting the name of Jesus, no matter the
circumstance. #JesusSwagger

~~~

The phrase, "The Holy Spirit led me to . . ." is a bold way to start any conversation. And while you may find some who will be receptive to your statement, you may also find many who are skeptical toward it.

I myself have had several different events where I firmly believe the Spirit told me to:

1. give my life to Christ;
2. get baptized;
3. preach and teach God's Word;
4. write books to help people deepen their faith;
5. help plant a church;
6. marry my wife;
7. try to adopt a child;
8. and move to Tennessee.

I look at each one of these events and realize they were not easy to accomplish. My wife lived across the country; I was twenty-two when I wrote my first book; I was twenty-one when I decided to pursue a church plant; I removed myself from my job, friends, and relationships when giving my life to Christ; and my wife and I hadn't even been married for a year before we were given the opportunity to pursue the adoption of a baby boy.

The Holy Spirit gave me the courage, wisdom, and peace I needed to pursue the things God had placed in my life. And the Spirit is working in this same way today. Using the phrase "The Holy Spirit told me to" is dangerous. But when it's truthful, it's both powerful and inspiring.

Most evangelical Christians hold widely varying viewpoints when it comes to the Holy Spirit, how he works within one's life, and whether or not he is still active today. If you take a moment to search the words *Holy Spirit* on the Internet, you are bound to come across thousands of controversial books, widely promoted conferences, faith-based blog posts, and pastoral sermons on the subject.

Much of the content can be split between two different groups: Christians who believe the Holy Spirit is alive, active, and manifesting the supernatural throughout our world; and Christians who believe in the Holy Spirit, see his actions to be alive, powerful, and audacious, but do not give in to the oversaturated attention he's been handed. They just don't believe the hype, and are very cautious about claiming he is still active the way he once was.

We have two different groups of individuals who

land on two different ends of the spiritual spectrum. One believes the Spirit is out front and socially active, while the other sees it working in the background, not looking for attention. The subject has brought Christian against Christian, pastor against pastor, church against church, and even denomination against denomination.

Many people will ask, "Well, who is right?" I'd like to think that they both are. I wouldn't call myself charismatic, nor would I call myself a conservative. But I would call myself someone who believes in the Trinity, and the living power of the Holy Spirit. To say the Holy Spirit is inactive in today's world would not only be unbiblical, but could also be looked at as heresy.

But before I get into what I see the Holy Spirit to be doing in the lives of Christians around the world, let me first take a look at who the Holy Spirit is and why he is among us.

THE TRINITY

The *Trinity* is a term used by most proclaimed Christians, but it's famously hard to explain in detail. While I believe the ideology behind the Trinity is too complex for our human brains to fully comprehend, I do believe the Trinity can be somewhat understood in a palatable way that makes a difference in each of our lives.

First off, the Trinity is composed of three different persons: the Father (God), Son (Jesus), and the Holy Spirit, who is also sometimes referred to as the Holy Ghost. That sounds scary to me, so I'd rather not refer to the Holy Spirit as ghost. And while all these persons come to make one awe-inspiring manifestation of the Godhead, they are three separate living persons who are all active in different ways.

John 1:1–4 states, "In the beginning was the Word, and the Word was with God, and the Word was God. He was with God in the beginning. Through him all things were made; without him nothing was made that has been made. In him was life, and that life was the light of all mankind" (NIV).

This verse gives an incredible picture of the Trinity, and it's a lot easier to spot than you think.

First, the author, John, refers to the relentless power of the Trinity as God, followed by the living manifestation of the Word as Jesus, and then the light of man as God's guiding light known as the Holy Spirit. Each person of the Trinity has individual characteristics and responsibilities, yet they never act independently or in opposition to one another. They have complete understanding between themselves.

Trinity, as defined by *Merriam Webster* dictionary, is "the union of the three divine persons (Father, Son and Holy Spirit) in one Godhead."[22] Martin H. Manser describes the Holy Spirit as, "The co-equal and co-eternal Spirit of the Father and the Son, who inspired Scripture and brings new life to the people of God. The Spirit of

God is often portrayed in Scripture in terms of 'breath,' 'life' or 'wind,' indicating his role in sustaining and bringing life to God's creation."[23]

Regardless of where you look for a definition, the Holy Spirit is basically the living, breathing, life-bringing manifestation of God in each of our individual lives. I believe the Holy Spirit to be in the business of exalting the name of Jesus, no matter the circumstance (John 16:12–14). The discussion at hand isn't whether or not the Holy Spirit is alive, but whether or not the Spirit is working in the ways people are claiming he does.

When you hear the term *Holy Spirit*, what is the first thing that comes to your mind? For most people it's the concept of speaking in tongues, Spirit-slaying televangelists, and supernatural healings. And although I don't believe the Holy Spirit has any limitations, I do believe the Holy Spirit isn't in the business of trying to prove a point. Frankly, he doesn't need to.

I'm not saying the Spirit of God is opposed to consuming one's body, providing supernatural healings, or even raising someone from the dead. We must understand, though, that we ourselves do not control the Holy Spirit; instead, the Holy Spirit is controlled by the power and will of God.

Charles Stanley made the distinction this way: "Earthly wisdom is 'doing what comes naturally' . . . Godly wisdom is doing what the Holy Spirit compels us to do."[24]

THE SPIRIT DID WHAT?

Many of the pentecostal and charismatic movements announce the Holy Spirit as someone who is alive, living with our bodies, and allowing us to manifest his power on a daily basis. This stance has brought much controversy to the movements, even leading other Christian leaders to describe their members as unbiblical, or not true Christians.

And while I believe those statements are extremely harsh and ill-thought, I do believe there will always be individuals who dramatize and embellish what the Spirit is actually doing. But hey, people will always do that sort of thing. As long as one isn't preaching contrary to biblical truth, there's no real problem in getting excited. The problem is found when people focus more on the acts of the Spirit than they do on the grace, salvation, and love of Jesus (Matthew 7:20–23).

Many see all the healings, the prophecy, and the spectacular acts of the Spirit that these movements focus on as false and not aligned with biblical text. Statements like "the Spirit doesn't work that way anymore" are par for the course, and many individuals completely tune out the overall idea of the Spirit performing the miraculous signs and wonders that these believers are claiming.

Even though my personal Christian practices may not align completely with some of these movements, who am I to say what the Holy Spirit can and can't do? Yes, there are some who take advantage of the idea and run past sanity, but that doesn't mean you should be suspicious of everyone who talks about the Spirit. These people are still your brothers and sisters in Christ. We're still the church, regardless of our differences.

Just because you've never seen the Spirit heal the blind or raise someone from the dead, doesn't mean it's not true. None of us have seen oxygen before, yet we still believe in it. How is this any different?

The second we start claiming what the Holy Spirit can and can't do is the second we've forfeited the true power of God, and made it into something that we can manipulate or control. That just isn't the case.

There are many things about God, Jesus, and the Holy Spirit that we may never be able to fully understand, but that doesn't mean we should stop believing or seeking to understand. If God was small enough to understand, he wouldn't be big enough to call God.

John 14:26 describes the function of the Holy Spirit: "But the Helper, the Holy Spirit, whom the Father will send in my name, he will teach you all things and bring to your remembrance all that I have said to you" (ESV).

In the New Testament, the Holy Spirit is active in those who call themselves followers of Jesus. The term *Holy Spirit* is used around 142 times depending on what version you read; there is obviously no hiding the truth of his existence, and God's Word shows that he is active.

The Bible contains many different names for the Holy Spirit. Some of them include:

- the Lord (2 Thessalonians 3:5)
- Power of the Highest (Luke 1:35 KJV)
- Spirit of God (Genesis 1:2; 1 Corinthians 2:11)
- Eternal Spirit (Hebrews 9:14)
- Comforter (John 14:16 KJV)
- Guide (John 16:13)
- Spirit of counsel (Isaiah 11:2)
- Spirit of holiness (Romans 1:4 KJV)
- Spirit of revelation (Ephesians 1:17 KJV)
- Helper (John 14:26 ESV)
- Witness (Revelation 1:5)

He's there, obviously, so why do so many ignore him?

I think people are afraid. We are afraid of what might happen if we allow his power into our lives—we're afraid of what might have to change, or what we might lose, not thinking of what we might gain. Many of us put our fear of the unknown in front of the power and potential of the Holy Spirit. It's sad to think that we could be turning from the Spirit's prompting due to a wall of fear. Fear is a liar, and the Spirit brings us the truth (John 16:13).

QUENCHING THE SPIRIT

I've noticed that many people get a little uncomfortable when you talk about the Holy Spirit, and part of me associates this with so many not truly investing in his power and guidance. Paul wrote to the Thessalonians,

"Do not quench the Spirit. Do not treat prophecies with contempt but test them all; hold on to what is good, reject every kind of evil" (1 Thessalonians 5:19–22 NIV).

I don't believe you can be a Christian while quenching the Spirit of God—while ignoring your conscience, while pretending as though God can't actively speak to you. It's like saying you want some ice without the part where it's made of water. And while many people embellish and focus solely on the works of the Spirit, I believe there is a whole different side that could be seen as not giving enough credit and validity to him.

I can't imagine my life without God, Jesus, and the Holy Spirit. They all come in one package. You don't get to pick and choose based on your preference. It's all or nothing. Even though this may seem pretty obvious, many people very rarely discuss the Holy Spirit's movement and activeness in their lives. It's almost as if people don't want to believe in something they can't actually control. Instead we want to focus on subjects that are more comfortable to discuss. Many people would claim that this outlook is unbiblical as well. When we only discuss the works of man and ignore the unexplainable, we are telling God we don't believe in the power of his Spirit.

So which is it? Who is right? Do I allow the Holy Spirit to heal the sick and give sight to the blind? Or, do I view the Holy Spirit as the guiding light of Jesus, and see him as one who doesn't work the way he used to?

Truthfully, I believe it's both.

The idea that the Holy Spirit can only work in one unique way smothers any claim of him being part of the all-powerful God. If the Spirit is truly the working hand of Jesus, the Spirit can do and will do what he pleases in each and every individual. Some may pray in tongues, and some may keep their mouths shut. Some may worship through song and dance, while others may worship through quiet and tranquility. Some may teach verse by verse, while others may preach topically and thematically. The truth is that we are all different people who have been called to live different and unique lives.

The Holy Spirit can work in many different ways. Just because the Holy Spirit is working in your life differently than he is another's doesn't mean that the other individual is wrong or outside the will of God. We're all unique, have different sets of fingerprints, and have different callings from God, so of course the Spirit is going to work differently in each of us.

R. A. Torrey said in his book *The Person and Work of the Holy Spirit*, "A true Christian life is a personally conducted life, conducted at every turn by a Divine Person. It is the believer's privilege to be absolutely set free from all care and worry and anxiety as to the decisions which we must make at any turn of life. The Holy Spirit undertakes all that responsibility for us. A true Christian life is not one governed by a long set of rules without us, but led by a living and ever-present Person within us."[25]

We can see that, in Torrey's estimation, the Holy Spirit is actively conducting the lifestyle of each and every person. The Holy Spirit is said to undertake the responsibility of guiding great decisions for us, relieving us of having to completely govern our own lives. I love Torrey's words here because they ascribe to the Holy Spirit complete and utter control of our lives as Christians, rather than leaving them all up to the control of our feeble words and decisions. Sure, the power of the Holy Spirit can be encouraged through the words of our faith, but it's not us who has complete control—it's someone much bigger.

When viewing the Spirit's activity throughout the world, we begin to see that differences such as personalities, zip codes, states, countries, and levels of faith are not hindrances to what the Holy Spirit does and doesn't do. There is no cookie-cutter doctrine when it comes to what he's capable of. It's simply not our call.

All around the world you will find stories and testimonies of people who have been healed, redeemed, and rescued thanks to the Spirit of God. And while many people might sit in the comfort of their homes and say, "That's not true," I would encourage them to step out into the world and open up their hearts' guidance to the Spirit of God, and not what only their minds can fathom.

Acts 2:1–13 portrays a scene I find powerful and comedic, as the Spirit takes control of a group of believers on the day of Pentecost, leaving others in confusion.

The day of Pentecost comes ten days after the ascension of Jesus into heaven, about fifty days after Easter, and is referred to by many as the birthday of the church. The biblical account in Acts 2 tells the story:

> When the day of Pentecost came, they were all together in one place. Suddenly a sound like the blowing of a violent wind came from heaven and filled the whole house where they were sitting. They saw what seemed to be tongues of fire that separated and came to rest on each of them. All of them were filled with the Holy Spirit and began to speak in other tongues as the Spirit enabled them.
>
> Now there were staying in Jerusalem God-fearing Jews from every nation under heaven. When they heard this sound, a crowd came together in bewilderment, because each one heard their own language being spoken. Utterly amazed, they asked: "Aren't all these who are speaking Galileans? Then how is it that each of us hears them in our native language? Parthians, Medes and Elamites; residents of Mesopotamia, Judea and Cappadocia, Pontus and Asia, Phrygia and Pamphylia, Egypt and the parts of Libya near Cyrene; visitors from Rome (both Jews and converts to Judaism); Cretans and Arabs—we hear them declaring the wonders of God in our own tongues!" Amazed and perplexed, they asked one another, "What does this mean?"

Some, however, made fun of them and said, "They have had too much wine." (vv. 1–13 NIV)

Even in the early days of the church, the power and activity of the Holy Spirit wasn't truly understood. If people in biblical times thought that those who were being used by the Spirit were drunk, I can't imagine what kinds of things people are saying in this day and age.

Not everyone is going to understand what the Spirit does or doesn't do in your life. Initiating your Jesus swagger starts by first admitting that you need the Spirit to live out the true life of a Christian. True freedom, confidence, and spiritual effectiveness simply can't exist without him.

A Christian without the Holy Spirit is like a cheeseburger without the cheese. It's not what it claims to be.

CHAPTER 8

JESUS IS NOT YOUR HOMEBOY

Jesus isn't looking to be your friend.
He's looking to be much more than that.
#JesusSwagger

~~~

In the mid 2000s, the phrase "Jesus is my homeboy" started trending among evangelical Christians, and soon began finding its way onto T-shirts, hats, and other personal accessories. The origination of the phrase had a powerful meaning: it was meant to signify that Jesus wanted to relate to people personally. But the use of it in today's evangelical culture often comes off as shallow, flaky, even irreverent. While this cute saying seems harmless and fun, the attitude that it stands for can actually be a detriment to a deepening relationship with God. Why, you ask?

Because Jesus deserves more honor and respect than the term *homeboy* credits him. And while many people think calling Jesus their homeboy makes him look more inviting to nonbelievers, it's more likely presenting a fake image of who Jesus really is. Yes, Jesus can be described as many different things, but I don't think *homeboy* is something that magnifies the importance of his being.

Your childhood best friend is your homeboy. Your favorite barista is your homeboy. Jesus, however, is *not* your homeboy: he is your Father, your Savior, your Redeemer, your Rock, your Salvation, your Lord, your Christ, your Shield, your Protector, your Friend, and so much more.

Is using that terminology wrong? No. But is it honoring his true nature? Not even remotely close.

In everything we do, we are called to show honor and respect to the one we call Savior (1 Corinthians 6:20). While there are many names to describe the God of the universe, I don't think *homeboy* should be one of them. It's as if I were to refer to Jesus as *dude* or *bro*. My own father would find that odd, let alone my heavenly father.

We're living in a world that seems to become less and less faithful as the years go by. The Barna Group states that 60 percent of teenagers will graduate high school without a grasp of their faithful roots.[26] And while the number of faithful servants is decreasing, we need to make sure that the recognition and adoration we have for Jesus continues to increase. We're called to be different, after all (2 Corinthians 6:17).

THE FEAR OF GOD

The term *God-fearing* is something many Christians do not like to use with today's generation. And while many people see "fear" as an inaccurate description of their relationship with God, the Bible itself says otherwise.

Proverbs 1:7 explains, "The fear of the LORD is the beginning of knowledge, but fools despise wisdom and instruction" (NIV). *Fear* is not the same as being scared in this context: it's being rightly aware of God's magnitude, and letting it affect us seriously. In this verse, we can see that the fear of the Lord is promised to bring wisdom and knowledge. That's the healthy kind of fear.

I encourage you not to see this as a literal fear like that of a nightmare, but instead as honor and reverence for our heavenly father. Sort of in the way one could fear the presence of a boss, parent, or police officer, one should fear the Lord, but obviously in a deeper and more admiring form.

Jim Newheiser describes our fear of God this way:

> To fear God is to regard God with reverent awe. He alone is holy, awesome, and glorious (Isa. 6:3). He is worthy of our respect. Because God is righteous, we should be concerned about the consequences of displeasing him. Our fear is not one which leaves us cowering and terrified but rather is like the respect a son should have towards his father. The fear of God leads to wise and pure living: "By the fear of the Lord one keeps away from evil" (Prov. 16:6).
>
> To fear God is to submit to him, turning from self-assertion and evil: "Do not be wise in your own eyes; fear the Lord and turn away from evil" (3:7). We are not autonomous beings, free to assert our own will

and decide what is right for us. We must acknowledge the Lord's sovereign moral governance of the universe. We should be open to his training and correction and trust that his way is always best. To fear God is to know God. To know God is to have life (19:23a). When you fear God, you no longer fear men (29:25).

The fear of the Lord is not a beginning like the first stage of a rocket which is cast aside after it has served its purpose. Rather, the fear of the Lord is the beginning of wisdom in the same way in which a foundation is the beginning of a house: everything that comes after the foundation is built upon it.[27]

A literal fear of God should not be the reason of your obedience. Instead, obedience comes out of honor, respect, and admiration for his being. The idea of referring to God or Jesus as your homeboy completely throws out any form of true respect, and instead paints them as nothing more than an acquaintance or pal.

FEAR BUILT THE ARK

The story of Noah's Ark is one that all of us read as children. And while many of us may look at this story as being overtold and overused (and overly made into toys and storybooks and kids' bedroom decorations), there is actually a hidden message about fearing God that is very relevant to what we're talking about. The Bible begins the story by describing a world that seems alarmingly familiar to ours: "Now the earth was corrupt in God's sight and was full of violence. God saw how corrupt the earth had become, for all the people on earth had corrupted their ways" (Genesis 6:11–13 NIV).

Then God came up with a plan to push the reset button, and he told Noah, "I am going to put an end to all people, for the earth is filled with violence because of them. I am surely going to destroy both them and the earth" (v. 13 NIV).

Terrifying, right? God proceeds to lay out detailed instructions to Noah. Any other person might have taken shortcuts, or tried to "improve" on God's plan, or even said "This is absolute craziness" and just ignored God. Or they would have quaked in fear at the prospect of the world ending, and rushed to obey God in order to save their skin. But Noah *feared* God in the way that we're talking about—he respected the righteousness behind his plan so much, and took him so seriously, that he followed all his instructions to the inch (or to the cubit).

Then came the instructions for building the ark:

"The ark is to be three hundred cubits long, fifty cubits wide and thirty cubits high. Make a roof for it, leaving below the roof an opening one cubit high all around. Put a door in the side of the ark and make lower, middle and upper decks ... You are to bring into the ark two of all living creatures, male and female, to keep them alive with you. Two of every kind of bird, of every kind of animal and of every kind of creature that moves along the ground will come to you to be kept alive. You are to take every kind of food that is to be eaten and store it away as food for you and for them." Noah did everything *just as God commanded him.* (Genesis 6:15–22 NIV, emphasis added)

Noah takes all of God's direction into account, and in time constructs a ship that I believe would be marveled at by any of today's architects. That's not only because of the ark's size and stature, but because of the limited tools at Noah's disposal.

The writer of Hebrews in the New Testament also used Noah as an example of someone who properly feared God: as a man who followed his commands and respected his being.

By faith Noah, when warned about things not yet seen, in *holy* fear built an ark to save his family. By his faith he condemned the world and became heir of the righteousness that is in keeping with faith. (Hebrews 11:7 NIV, emphasis added)

When I read this passage, I don't see a man who built an ark because he was afraid. Instead I see a man who respected and valued the Lord's wisdom so much that he took into account everything the Lord was guiding him to do.

One of Merriam Webster's definitions of fear is "to expect or worry about (something bad or unpleasant)."[28] When someone loves you and has the best intentions for you, you don't fear them in the way this definition describes—expecting disaster. Sure, Noah was facing disaster, but he expected God to honor his covenant and save him and his family. He feared God because God was powerful and worthy. The root of the word *fear* is the Hebrew word *Yare,* which means "to fear, reverence, honor, respect."[29]

God deserves that kind of honor from us. God isn't a tyrant, and neither is he a pushover. He is the perfect combination of tough and tender. Flawless in every way.

When it comes to your relationship with him, take into consideration the power and magnitude of his being, but also the comfort and peace he offers as Lord. God isn't in the business of scaring people into submission, but he may be willing to flex a little to show you what he's made of.

BRINGING HONOR BACK

The idea of honoring God has slowly fallen off the map over the last few decades. There was once a time when going to church weekly was seen as important, when praying was taken seriously, and when honoring God was on the top of many people's priority lists.

One might ask, where has all the honor gone? But I don't think honor has really left. We give plenty of honor and respect—but we give it to things other than Jesus himself. Relationships, money, and popularity are all things our culture gives honor to on a daily basis. Then there's image, success—take your pick.

When our relationship with God becomes more like a trend and less like a lifestyle, when it starts playing second fiddle to whatever else we've got going on in our lives, we've begun treating Jesus more like our homeboy than our Lord. I don't believe God intended us to bring Jesus down to a level where he is nothing more than another buddy. Yes, Jesus wants to be our friend. But no, Jesus doesn't want things to stay that way. John 5:23 states, "That all may honor the Son just as they honor the Father. Whoever does not honor the Son does not honor the Father, who sent him" (NIV). If we find ourselves showing little to no honor to Jesus, we are also refusing to honor his Father, God. We are refusing to fear him.

In the biblical sense, honor and fear go hand in hand with one another. When you fear God, you honor God. And when you honor God, you in turn are fearing God. Variations of the word *honor* are found throughout the King James Bible around 170 times. A relationship with God, Jesus, and the Holy Spirit cannot exist without honor. It's more than just an attribute of our spiritual relationship; it's an entire way of living.

In the same way the Bible commands us to honor

our mothers and fathers, I believe God is looking for us to honor him through all aspects of our lives. This can be done in many ways, but definitely the most prominent would be through our time, energy, words, actions, worship, and thoughts—and in putting him above all material objects and other goals. We honor him with the music we listen to, the movies we watch, the things we eat, and even the stuff we spend our money on. If we do everything in a way that reflects the majesty and purity of God's nature, we are in turn honoring him with all that we are, and inviting him to direct our lives

IN FEAR AND FAITH

You remember the story of Jesus walking on water, and Peter coming to him on the lake? Matthew 14 tells us that Peter was a man who was willing to step off a boat, into the raging water, all in order to reach Jesus amid rough winds and crashing waves. While the rest of his friends looked on in terror, faithful Peter stepped off the edge of a boat without looking back.

Way too many scholars and theologians give Peter a bad rap for doing something so foolish, and for losing faith halfway out and sinking: "But when he saw the wind, he was afraid and, beginning to sink, cried out, 'Lord, save me!'" (Matthew 14:30 NIV). But Peter did something not many of us would do ourselves. He was audaciously faithful, and went over the edge.

It's not just Peter's faith that allowed him to walk on water for a brief moment, but also the fear he had for God and his son Jesus. Peter didn't step off because he was afraid of the Lord, but instead because he had reverent fear for the Lord based on the time they'd spent together. Here is how it happened:

> Immediately Jesus made the disciples get into the boat and go on ahead of him to the other side, while he dismissed the crowd. After he had dismissed them, he went up on a mountainside by himself to pray. Later that night, he was there alone, and the boat was already a considerable distance from land, buffeted by the waves because the wind was against it.
>
> Shortly before dawn Jesus went out to them, walking on the lake. When the disciples saw him walking on the lake, they were terrified. "It's a ghost," they said, and cried out in fear.
>
> But Jesus immediately said to them: "Take courage! It is I. Don't be afraid."
>
> "Lord, if it's you," Peter replied, "tell me to come to you on the water."
>
> "Come," he said. Then Peter got down out of the boat, walked on the water and came toward Jesus. (Matthew 14:22–29 NIV)

Jesus told them to not be afraid, and Peter took him at his word. Then, embarrassingly, he got nervous and started to sink. He took his eyes off Jesus for a minute and began to panic. The following is why people find it so easy to trash him:

> Immediately Jesus reached out his hand and caught him. "You of little faith," he said, "why did you doubt?" And when they climbed into the boat, the wind died down. Then those who were in the boat worshiped him, saying, "Truly you are the Son of God." (Matthew 14:31–33 NIV)

Peter's "little faith" may have caused him to go down, but a healthy fear and honor set him on a pathway of faith in the first place. That's more than what most can claim. It was only because of the voice and command of Jesus that Peter accepted his fate of stepping off the wooden platform his feet were on.

Although Peter found his miracle-moment short-lived, he still accomplished what he set out to do. He found himself moving closer to the presence of Jesus, and in the end it's what saved him from being lost in the water.

Fearing God and stepping out will instill a way of life that will not only supercharge your faith, but give you a peace and understanding that is beyond anything this world can offer (Philippians 4:7). Fearing God is the essence of our Christian faith. Without fear, we will fail.

Oswald Chambers said it best when he wrote, "The remarkable thing about fearing God is that when you fear

God, you fear nothing else, whereas if you do not fear God, you fear everything else."[30]

Increase your fear for God, and you will decrease your fear of everything life throws at you. When we put God in the highest seat in our lives, everything else will seem small and inadequate compared to his glory.

AFRAID TO BE AFRAID

As a Christian, I find that some of the easiest traps for me to fall into are the ones I have set for myself. Sometimes, the hardest things for me to overcome are the walls I have built with my own hands. And the hardest addictions to conquer are the ones I have subconsciously nourished. It's my lack of fear and faith in Jesus that puts me into a position of trying to do things on my own. Human nature tells me to trust myself, while faith in Jesus tells me to not trust my sinful nature.

It's fairly easy to get in a habit of doing things your way, on your time, and for your benefit. But that is the exact opposite of who Jesus Christ has called us to be.

As Christians, we are not the directors of our lives anymore. We gave up that right the second we decided to give our lives to him. In reality, we are supporting actors who have been blessed with the opportunity to be part of God's bigger story. When we begin directing our lives the way that we see fit, we will begin to lose touch with our heavenly Father. That intimate and personal connection is the very thing that keeps us focused on righteousness and turned away from worldliness.

Stay focused on your role as a supporting actor, and allow God to direct your life in the way he sees fit. It's not about us. Trust me, if he can create the world, I'm sure he's more than capable of directing your life. Just like Peter, you and I are called to step off our boats and into the will of God's direction. "In all your ways submit to him, and he will make your paths straight" (Proverbs 3:6 NIV).

FEAR CONQUERED THE CROWD

Imagine being sick, alone, fearful, and viewed as nothing more than a living infection by the people around you. Imagine not being able to visit your family, see your parents, or ever spend time with any of your friends. Imagine being treated like you don't even exist, while pets and farm animals are given more adequate living quarters than you are.

While this may be hard to imagine, this was the broken life of a fragile woman living in Galilee. And while she sat on her mat, overtaken with a sickness that condemned her as unclean, the busy city life went on without her.

This woman who had been subject to bleeding for twelve years considered her worth nothing more than what those who passed her by told her it was. I can only imagine that the slurs thrown at her were nothing short of detestable. She was mocked, mimicked, bullied, and taken for every penny she had by doctors who claimed to have a cure to make her better.

When we look at the concept of fearing God and relate it to this woman, we can see that the only fear she possessed was for those who mocked her. She feared that any day she could be banished from the city, asked never to return again. And she feared that death might reach her body before a cure would.

While this bleeding woman sat on her mat and dwindled in her sorrows, she began hearing of a man who was known to heal the sick, give sight to the blind, and raise the dead to life. She remembered conversations she had overheard of a man named Jesus. While a spark of hope kindled in her heart, she could hear the crowds of people following and cheering for what could only have been Jesus himself.

I imagine her thought process was that of a child. *If I could only get to Jesus, I bet he can make everything better.*

And with hope in her heart and the fear of the Lord's power as her courage, she made her way toward the man who was said could make her clean again.

Now when Jesus returned, a crowd welcomed him, for they were all expecting him. Then a man named Jairus, a synagogue leader, came and fell at Jesus' feet, pleading with him to come to his house because his only daughter, a girl of about twelve, was dying.

As Jesus was on his way, the crowds almost crushed him. And a woman was there who had been subject to bleeding for twelve years, but no one could heal her. She came up behind him and touched the edge of his cloak, and immediately her bleeding stopped.

"Who touched me?" Jesus asked. When they all denied it, Peter said, "Master, the people are crowding and pressing against you." But Jesus said, "Someone touched me; I know that power has gone out from me." Then the woman, seeing that she could not go unnoticed, came trembling and fell at his feet. In the presence of all the people, she told why she had touched him and how she had been instantly healed. Then he said to her, "Daughter, your faith has healed you. Go in peace." (Luke 8:40–48 NIV)

I get chills when reading this passage: a woman who thought she had no future was miraculously healed by a man claiming to be the Son of God. Jesus healed the woman, called upon her, and then told her, "Daughter, your faith has healed you. Go in peace."

Not only did the woman find the courage to get up off her mat and seek Jesus, but her fear of God was enough to give her faith in his son Jesus. In doing this, the woman broke through a crowd of people surrounding him, got on her hands and knees, and then managed to grab the tip of his robe. The moment she grabbed onto his robe, she was healed, made clean, and made new.

Notice the faith and admiration this woman had for God, Jesus, and the power of their being. Fear and faith intermingle in this passage. This woman feared the Lord in a way that broke through her lesser, worldly fear of those who were surrounding him. Her trembling fear is what led her closer to him, and her fear is what led to the cleansing of her body.

Let me ask you a question. What crowd are you pushing through? Many of us face crowds just like the one the bleeding woman faced. Instead of a literal crowd of people keeping you from the feet of Jesus, you instead could be faced with depression, anxiety, fear of rejection, fear of failure, financial hardships, or even insecurities. These "crowds," these fears, seem overwhelming, causing us to forget where the real power lies. If you're fearing all these other things, then you're not going to be able to fear God.

As William Gurnall said, "We fear men so much, because we fear God so little. One fear cures another. When man's terror scares you, turn your thoughts to the wrath of God."[31]

CONCLUSION

JESUS SWAGGER ISN'T OPTIONAL

Jesus swagger may be attractive. It may be life-giving. It may be a symptom of a heart devoted to God. But what it is not, is optional. The way you dress, love, act, and speak just can't go in opposition to the spirit of the One that died on a cross for your sins. Worldly swagger just doesn't fit you anymore.

On the other hand, if you've got God living in you and are seeking him truthfully—without posing—you cannot *help* but have Jesus swagger. It's a light that shines from you and makes people wonder what you've got.

So if your swagger has been something you've done on the surface to this point, I encourage you to ditch it. It wasn't doing you any good in the first place. You've got endless wells of the real stuff living inside you—if you have Christ inside you. Imagine no more slavery to image and others' judgment. Imagine knowing in your heart what really matters, and just not caring about the rest. Imagine not wasting time on that foolishness ever again.

The place that once held in your life is taken up by real, actual, world-changing purpose and a mission that comes straight from the Creator of the universe. Whatever swagger you develop as a side effect of that, well, that's a perk that shows the world where your priorities are.

By now, I hope you know for sure that we Christians don't have to go about life the way others do. We don't have to put on a show, say the right things, post all the right comments online, and act the part in our mannerisms and vocab. That's all just playing around. You, on the other hand, can walk with a holy swagger because you are in pursuit of a kingdom that is greater than anything this world can offer us.

We are called to be kingdom-chasing, love-wearing, grace-pouring soldiers of Christ. Yes, much of the world might not understand our motives. They were never meant to understand from the beginning. They were meant to be transformed. You and I have been set apart by a force that is beyond our wildest imagination. The One who created the heavens and the earth created us out of nothing but the dust we know to be under out feet. And then he gave us a job to do.

Jesus swagger comes from living a life that resembles nothing of ourselves, and has everything to do with the One who created us. It has nothing to do with how we fashion ourselves in the mirror. Our swagger is divine, holy, audacious, and graceful. It's a swagger unlike anything this world has ever seen. And I promise you it's something they will never forget.

ACKNOWLEDGMENTS

Jesus, your love and grace is what fuels me to live. I wouldn't be here today without your constant love and guidance.

ABOUT THE AUTHOR

Jarrid Wilson is a husband, millennial pastor, best-selling author, and inspirational blogger. His articles have been viewed by millions, showcased on some of today's hottest talk shows, and featured on national news stations worldwide. He is a dynamic speaker whose outside-the-box perspectives have gained him national recognition from some of today's most influential Christian leaders and pastors.

His highly unconventional way of sharing faith takes a fresh look at the way Jesus would call individuals to live out their everyday lives. Unafraid to tackle tough and controversial topics, Jarrid is known for his refreshing perspectives on what others may view as set in black-and-white. His blog is one of the most talked about faith-based blogs on the web, and his dedication to social media for the sake of faith has been paramount to his success as a writer.

Jarrid and his wife Juli live in Nashville, Tennessee, where Jarrid currently serves as the next-gen pastor of LifePoint Church.

NOTES

1. Snoop Dogg, "Boss's Life," *Tha Blue Carpet Treatment*, Geffen Records (2006).
2. Urban Dictionary, s.v. "swagger," definition 2, http://www.urbandictionary.com/define.php?term=swagger, accessed June 8, 2014.
3. Attributed to Mahatma Gandhi in W. P. King, review of *The Christ of the Indian Road*, by E. Stanley Jones, *Atlanta Constitution*, 7 February 1926, F14.
4. Francis Chan, *Crazy Love* (Colorado Springs: David C. Cook, 2013), 63.
5. Joseph Thayer and G. Abbot Smith, *The NAS New Treatment Greek Lexicon*, s.v. "Ginosko," http://www.biblestudytools.com/lexicons/greek/nas/.
6. Matthew Henry, *Commentary on the Whole Bible* (1706), http://www.biblestudytools.com/commentaries/matthew-henry-complete/.
7. *Strong's Concordance*, s.v. "ekptuó," http://biblehub.com/greek/1609.htm.

8. Martin Luther, *The Communion of the Christian With God*, trans. Wilhelm Herrmann (London: Williams & Norgate, 1906), 332.

9. Origen, *Commentary on the Epistle to the Romans, Books 6–10*, trans. Thomas P. Scheck (Washington, DC: Catholic University of America Press, 2002), 228.

10. R. Kent Hughes, *Romans: Righteousness From Heaven* (Wheaton, IL: Crossway, 1991), 250–51.

11. Centers for Disease Control and Prevention, "National Marriage and Divorce Rate Trends," National Vital Statistics System, last updated February 19, 2013, http://www.cdc.gov/nchs/nvss/marriage_divorce_tables.htm.

12. Mother Teresa, *No Greater Love* (Novato: New World Library, 2001), 69.

13. K. J. Bryer, "Mother Teresa," in James Dixon Douglas and Philip Wesley Comfort eds., *Who's Who in Christian History* (Wheaton, IL: Tyndale House, 1992).

14. Abigail Van Buren, "Dear Abby," *Park City Daily News*, April 1, 1964, p. 3.

15. Charles Wood, *Sermon Outlines on Great Doctrinal Themes* (Grand Rapids: Kregel Publications, 1991), 15.

16. Of disputed origin, a paraphrase often attributed to Mahatma Ghandi.

17. C. S. Lewis, *Mere Christianity* (New York: Touchstone, 1996), 130–31.

18. Attributed to Alice Cooper, reportedly from a 2001 interview with the British *Sunday Times*.

19. NASA, "Failure is Not An Option," http://www.nasa.gov/multimedia/imagegallery/image_feature_2073.html.

20. From *Talladega Nights: The Ballad of Ricky Bobby* (Sony Pictures, 2006).

21. Tejvan Pettinger, "Dietrich Bonhoeffer," Biography Online, http://www.biographyonline.net/spiritual/dietrich-bonhoeffer.html.

22. *Merriam Webster Online*, s.v. "trinity," http://www.merriam-webster.com/dictionary/trinity.

23. Martin H. Manser, ed., *Dictionary of Bible Themes Scripture Index*, s.v. "3010 God, the Holy Spirit," available on BibleGateway.com, https://www.biblegateway.com/resources/dictionary-of-bible-themes/3010-God-Holy-Spirit.

24. Charles Stanley, *God's Way Day by Day* (New York: HarperCollins Christian Publishers, 2007), 112.

25. R. A. Torrey, *The Person and Work of the Holy Spirit* (New York: Cosimo, repr. 1997), 112.

26. "Most Twentysomethings Put Christianity on the Shelf Following Spiritually Active Teen Years," Barna Group, 2009, https://www.barna.org/barna-update/article/16-teensnext-gen/147-most-twentysomethings-put-christianity-on-the-shelf-following-spiritually-active-teen-years#.U_gpFbywKFk.

27. Jim Newheiser, *Opening up Proverbs* (Leominster: Day One Publications, 2008), 28.

28. *Merriam-Webster Online*, s.v. "fear," http://www.merriam-webster.com/dictionary/fear.

29. *The NAS Old Testament Hebrew Lexicon*, s.v. "Yare,'" Strong's Number 3372, BibleStudyTools.com, http://www.biblestudytools.com/lexicons/hebrew/nas/yare.html.

30. Oswald Chambers, quoted in Martin H. Manser ed., *The Westminster Collection of Christian Quotations* (Louisville: Westminster John Knox, 2001), 322.

31. William Gurnall, quoted in Martin H. Manser, ed., *The Westminster Collection of Christian Quotations* (Westminster: John Knox Press, 2001), 109.